CGP
– books
like no others!

Really
Important Stuff
The Revision Gu...

CGP

<u>Achieve mastery of KS2 Maths with CGP!</u>

This book is perfect for stretching pupils aged 10-11 who are getting to grips with the Year 6 Maths objectives quickly and confidently.

It's packed with challenging new ways to approach each Year 6 topic, all explained with crystal-clear study notes and step-by-step examples.

We've also included plenty of open-ended enrichment questions to get them thinking independently about each topic, plus practice questions (with answers) to test the key skills at the end of each section!

<u>What CGP is all about</u>

Our sole aim here at CGP is to produce the highest quality books — carefully written, immaculately presented and dangerously close to being funny.

Then we work our socks off to get them out to you — at the cheapest possible prices.

Contents

Published by CGP

Contributor:
Stephanie Burton

Editors:
Shaun Harrogate, Ceara Hayden, David Ryan.

ISBN: 978 1 78294 581 9

With thanks to Alison Griffin and Dawn Wright for the proofreading.
With thanks to Laura Jakubowski for the copyright research.

Thumb illustration used throughout the book © iStockphoto.com.

Contains public sector information licensed under the Open Government Licence v3.0.
http://www.nationalarchives.gov.uk/doc/open-government-licence/

Printed by Elanders Ltd, Newcastle upon Tyne.
Clipart from Corel®

Based on the classic CGP style created by Richard Parsons.

About This Book

This Book has All the Topics for Year 6...

Each page of this book covers a <u>different topic</u>, with <u>examples</u> to help <u>explain</u> the maths.

This book covers the <u>Attainment Targets</u> for <u>Year 6</u> of the <u>2015 National Curriculum</u>.

... but We've Made them More Challenging

The content of each page <u>enriches</u> what you already know about the topic to really <u>stretch</u> your brain. By <u>deepening</u> your understanding, this book provides a <u>challenging</u> and <u>interesting</u> approach to Year 6 maths.

You'll find <u>enrichment questions</u> like these throughout the book — they get you to think <u>more deeply</u> about what you've just learned, look for <u>alternative methods</u> and provide a starting point for your own <u>investigations</u>.

? Why is it difficult to compare pie charts when you <u>don't know</u> their totals?

At the end of each section there are <u>practice questions</u>. You can see what you know and what you don't know.

This Study Book has a <u>matching Question Book</u>. It's got <u>questions</u> on all the topics, <u>open-ended investigations</u> to really dive deep into the maths and some <u>tests</u> too.

There are Learning Objectives on All Pages

The Learning Objectives say <u>what you should already be able to do</u>.

<u>Printable checklists</u> of all the objectives can be found at www.cgpbooks.co.uk/primarymaths.

I can win gold at the Olympics.

Use the <u>tick circles</u> to show how <u>confident</u> you feel with the <u>challenging maths</u> on the page.

Tick here if you need a bit more practice with this challenging maths.

If you found the maths on this page too tricky, tick here.

Tick this circle if you can do all the challenging maths on the page.

"I can multiply a four-digit number by a two-digit number."

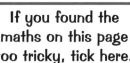

Place Value in Very Large Numbers

A Million is 1000 Times Bigger Than a Thousand

Here's a recap of the names of the columns in large numbers:

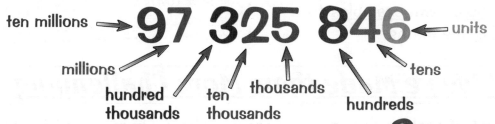

ten millions → **97 325 846** ← units

millions, hundred thousands, ten thousands, thousands, hundreds, tens

Each place is <u>ten times bigger</u> than the place to its <u>right</u> and <u>ten times smaller</u> than the place to its <u>left</u>.

? What place do you think comes to the left of ten millions?

EXAMPLES:

① <u>Draw an arrow</u> on the number line pointing to <u>1 400 000</u>.

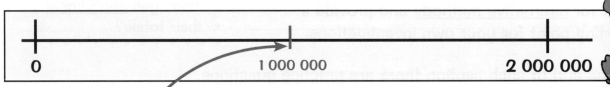

0   1 000 000   2 000 000

1. Draw a line <u>halfway</u> between 0 and 2 000 000 to mark out 1 000 000.

2. Divide the gap from 1 000 000 to 2 000 000 into <u>10 equal steps</u>. Each step is worth $(2\,000\,000 - 1\,000\,000) \div 10 = \underline{100\,000}$.

3. Finally, count <u>4 steps</u> from 1 000 000 to get to <u>1 400 000</u>.

? What would each step be worth if you divided the gap into 2, 5 or 20 equal steps?

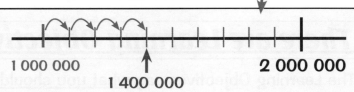

1 000 000   2 000 000

1 400 000

② <u>Estimate</u> the <u>number</u> that the arrow below is pointing to.

20 000 000   30 000 000

1. Each <u>small step</u> is worth $(30\,000\,000 - 20\,000\,000) \div 4 = 2\,500\,000$.

2. So <u>half</u> a small step is worth $2\,500\,000 \div 2 = 1\,250\,000$.

3. The arrow is <u>one and a half</u> small steps <u>above</u> 20 000 000, so <u>add on</u>: $20\,000\,000 + 2\,500\,000 + 1\,250\,000 = \underline{23\,750\,000}$.

"I can read, write, order and compare numbers up to ten million."

Rounding Whole Numbers

Rounding Whole Numbers

If a whole number has been rounded to the nearest ten, hundred or thousand, the actual number could be up to 5, 50 or 500 above or below the rounded number.

For example, a number that is 700 when rounded to the nearest hundred could be anywhere between 650 and 749:

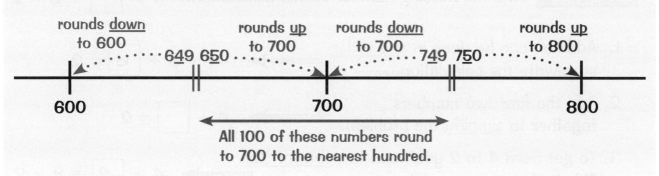

rounds down to 600 ···· 649 650 ···· rounds up to 700 ···· rounds down to 700 ···· 749 750 ···· rounds up to 800

600   700   800

All 100 of these numbers round to 700 to the nearest hundred.

? How many different whole numbers round to 70, to the nearest 10? What about 7000 to the nearest 1000? Can you see a pattern?

EXAMPLE:

4000 tickets have been sold to the International Teddy Bears' Picnic, to the nearest thousand tickets. Buzz has bought 4375 jars of honey, and wants to give one to each ticket-holder. Will this be enough?

1. Work out the largest whole number that rounds down to 4000 to the nearest thousand.

   | 4 | ? | ? | ? |

   First look at the decider — the digit in the hundreds column.

   If this digit is a 5, the number will round up to 5000. So it should be a 4.

2. Now fill in the other columns with the largest digits possible — 9's.

   | 4 | 4 | ? | ? |

3. So the largest whole number that will round down to 4000 is 4499.

   | 4 | 4 | 9 | 9 |

4. Buzz has 4375 jars of honey. 4375 < 4499, so there might not be enough honey for the largest number of ticket-holders.

"I can round any whole number."

Calculating With Negative Numbers

Finding Missing Numbers

Adding a negative number is the same as subtracting a positive number.

> 4 + –5 is the same as 4 – 5

You can use this to help you solve missing number problems.

EXAMPLE: Find the missing number in this calculation: –4 + ☐ + 8 = 2

1. Addition can be done in any order so rewrite the calculation. ⟹ –4 + 8 + 6 = 2

2. Add the first two numbers together to simplify the problem. ⟹ 4 + ☐ = 2

3. To get from 4 to 2 you need to subtract 2. This is the same as adding –2. ⟹ –4 + -2 + 8 = 2

EXAMPLE: Fill in the number square below so that all the rows, columns and diagonals add up to 0.

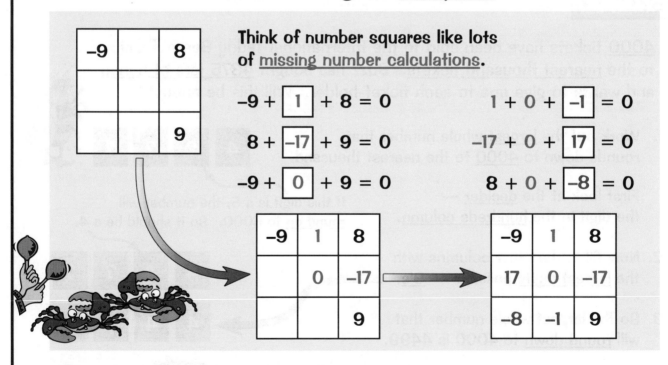

Think of number squares like lots of missing number calculations.

–9 + 1 + 8 = 0   1 + 0 + -1 = 0

8 + -17 + 9 = 0   –17 + 0 + 17 = 0

–9 + 0 + 9 = 0   8 + 0 + -8 = 0

? .... What do you notice about the completed number square? Can you make your own number square starting with different numbers in the three corners?

"I can calculate using negative numbers."

Solving Number Problems

There Might be More Than One Answer to a Question

With wordy questions, it's always good to check that you've fully answered the question — this might mean giving more than one answer.

EXAMPLE: Lee buys a bike. It costs £199, but the manager decreases the price by £5 for every scratch on the bike, then rounds the price to the nearest ten. Lee pays £160 for the bike. How many scratches could the bike have?

Find all the whole number amounts that round to £160 to the nearest ten.

£155 £156 £157 £158 £159
£160 £161 £162 £163 £164

Then check which ones can be made by subtracting multiples of £5 from £199.

£199 – (7 × £5) = £164
£199 – (8 × £5) = £159

So there could either be 7 scratches or 8 scratches on the bike.

There Might be Different Ways to Answer a Question

EXAMPLE:
Becky measured the temperature outside one morning, afternoon and evening. In the morning it was –3 °C. In the afternoon, it was 12 °C warmer than the morning. In the evening, it was 20 °C colder than the afternoon. What was the difference in temperature between the morning and evening?

There are different ways to tackle this question:

Work out the evening temperature...

–3 + 12 = 9 °C
9 – 20 = –11 °C

The difference between the morning temperature –3 °C and the evening temperature –11 °C was 8 °C.

OR

The temperature increased by 12 °C then decreased by 20 °C so the total change was...

12 – 20 = –8 °C

So the difference between the morning and evening temperatures was 8 °C.

? Can you think of another way which uses a diagram to help?

"I can solve number problems."

Practice Questions

1   Estimate the numbers that these arrows are pointing to.

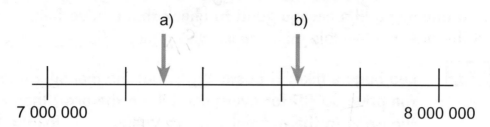

2   Dani is trying to choose a box of crayons to buy. There are four boxes to choose from but they all give different descriptions of how many crayons are inside.

Box	Number of Crayons	Highest Possible Number of Crayons	Lowest Possible Number of Crayons
A	500 (to the nearest 100)		
B	470 (to the nearest 10)		
C	476 exactly		
D	1000 (to the nearest 1000)		

a)   Copy and complete the table to show the highest and lowest possible values for the number of crayons inside each box.

b)   Can you say for sure which box has the most crayons inside?

3   Work out the missing values in the following:

a) $8 + \boxed{} = 4$ b) $\boxed{} + 32 = 16$ c) $-6 + \boxed{} + 21 = 4$

4   The temperature in Ulphabeck is −7 °C.
The difference in temperature between Ulphabeck and Wembleworth is 15 °C.

Work out the two possible temperatures in Wembleworth.

5   Georgio is thinking of a 2-digit whole number.

Both digits of Georgio's number are odd.
If you add the digits together you get 10.
The difference between the two digits is 4.

Find all the possible numbers that Georgio could be thinking of.

Written Multiplication

Work Out Missing Digits in a Calculation

Once you know how to do <u>long multiplication</u> using the <u>column method</u>, you can also work out <u>missing digits</u> in a calculation.

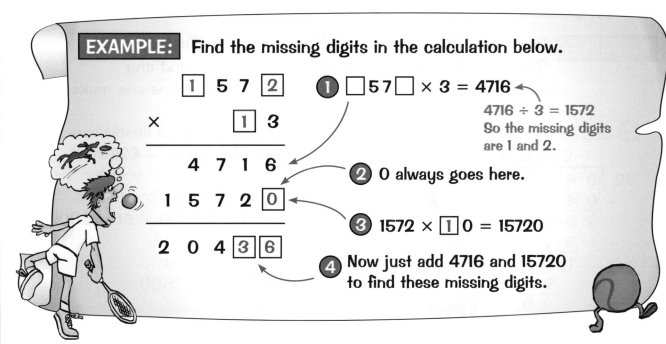

EXAMPLE: Find the missing digits in the calculation below.

$$
\begin{array}{r}
\boxed{1}\ 5\ 7\ \boxed{2} \\
\times\qquad \boxed{1}\ 3 \\
\hline
4\ 7\ 1\ 6 \\
1\ 5\ 7\ 2\ \boxed{0} \\
\hline
2\ 0\ 4\ \boxed{3}\ \boxed{6}
\end{array}
$$

1 $\boxed{}57\boxed{} \times 3 = 4716$

$4716 \div 3 = 1572$
So the missing digits are 1 and 2.

2 0 always goes here.

3 $1572 \times \boxed{1}0 = 15720$

4 Now just add 4716 and 15720 to find these missing digits.

EXAMPLE: Put the digits 1-6 into this calculation to make it correct. You can only use <u>each digit once</u>.

Use your knowledge of <u>column multiplication</u> to help you:

$\boxed{}\boxed{}\boxed{}\boxed{} \times \boxed{} = 6612$

This is the same as: $6612 \div \boxed{} = \boxed{}\boxed{}\boxed{}\boxed{}$

Try each digit from 1 to 6 in turn here.

$6612 \div 1 = 6612$
$6612 \div 2 = 3306$
$6612 \div 3 = 2204$
$6612 \div 4 = \underline{1653}$
$6612 \div 5 = 1322.4$
$6612 \div 6 = 1102$

$\underline{4}$ is the only value that gives no repeated digits in the answer, so the four-digit number is <u>1653</u>.

The only number left is <u>2</u>, so this must go in the remaining box.

$$
\begin{array}{r}
\boxed{}\ \boxed{}\ \boxed{}\ \boxed{} \\
\times\qquad \boxed{}\ \boxed{} \\
\hline
6\ 6\ 1\ 2 \\
3\ 3\ 0\ 6\ 0 \\
\hline
3\ 9\ 6\ 7\ 2
\end{array}
$$

So it must be <u>1653 × 24</u>. Check your answer.

? Can you think of other methods that you could use to find the missing digits in the two examples on this page?

"I can multiply a four-digit number by a two-digit number."

Written Division

Know What to do With Remainders

In <u>real-life</u> division problems, you'll often need to change a remainder to a <u>decimal</u> or <u>fraction</u>, or even <u>round</u> the answer up or down. Read the problem <u>carefully</u> to decide what you need to do.

EXAMPLE: Dorothy is dividing <u>8446</u> golf balls into bundles of <u>32</u>. She sells any complete bundles for <u>£10</u> each and any leftover balls for <u>£1</u> each. How much money does she make?

① Calculate 8446 ÷ 32.

```
        2 6 3 remainder 30
32 | 8 4 4 6
   - 6 4
     2 0 4
   - 1 9 2
       1 2 6
   -     9 6
         3 0
```

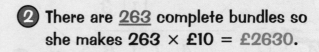

② There are <u>263</u> complete bundles so she makes 263 × £10 = £2630.

③ There are <u>30</u> balls left over so she makes another 30 × £1 = £30.

④ So in total she makes £2630 + £30 = <u>£2660</u>

? If you needed to buy exactly 83 golf balls from Dorothy, how much would it cost? Could you get a better deal if you bought more golf balls?

EXAMPLE: Selby divides <u>87</u> gobstoppers equally between his friends until he can't divide them any more. Each friend gets more than one and Selby is left with <u>6</u> gobstoppers. How many friends could he have?

STEP 1 — 87 − 6 = 81 gobstoppers divide equally between his friends — so find the factors of 81.

1, 3, 9, 27 and 81

STEP 2 — The number of friends needs to be <u>more than</u> the remainder — so it can't be 1 or 3.

1̶, 3̶, 9, 27, 8̶1̶ ← Each friend gets more than 1, so it can't be 81 either.

? Why does the number of friends need to be more than the remainder?

So Selby has either <u>9</u> or <u>27</u> friends.

"I can divide a four-digit number by a two-digit number and know what to do with remainders."

Mental Maths

Add and Subtract Big Numbers by Partitioning

To make big numbers easier to manage in your head, partition the number, then add or subtract the parts separately.

EXAMPLE: There were 17 254 buffalo roaming the grasslands in the spring. 2635 baby buffalo were born in summer. 367 ran away to greener pastures in the autumn. How many buffalo were left?

 Partition 2635 and add it in steps to 17 254.

$2635 = 2000 + 600 + 30 + 5$

$17\ 254 + 2000 + 600 + 30 + 5 = 19\ 889$

 Partition 367 and subtract it in steps from your answer.

$367 = 300 + 60 + 7$

$19\ 889 - 300 - 60 - 7 = 19\ 522$

There were 19 522 buffalo left.

Multiplying and Dividing Big Numbers

Multiplying and dividing big numbers in your head is much easier if you use partitioning again to help you out.

EXAMPLE: Work out 2113×5 in your head.

$2113 \times 5 = (2000 \times 5) + (100 \times 5) + (10 \times 5) + (3 \times 5)$

$= 10\ 000 + 500 + 50 + 15 = \underline{10\ 565}$

EXAMPLE: What is one quarter of 8236? Work it out in your head.

$8236 \div 4 = (8000 + 200 + 36) \div 4$ ← Split 8236 into thousands, hundreds and tens.

$= (8000 \div 4) + (200 \div 4) + (36 \div 4)$ ←

$= 2000 + 50 + 9 \boxed{= \underline{2059}}$ Then divide each number by 4.

? Why shouldn't you split up the division like this: $(8000 + 200 + 30 + 6) \div 4$? Can you think of another way of splitting it up that will work?

"I can solve number problems and do calculations with large numbers in my head."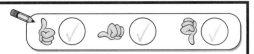

Estimating and Checking

Your Estimation Depends on How You Rounded

Estimating involves rounding. When <u>adding</u> or <u>multiplying</u>:

Rounding both numbers UP makes your estimation BIGGER than the real answer.
Rounding both numbers DOWN makes your estimation SMALLER than the real answer.

<u>BUT</u> things are different when <u>subtracting</u> or <u>dividing</u>:

Rounding the 1st number UP and the 2nd number DOWN makes your estimation BIGGER than the real answer.

Rounding the 1st number DOWN and the 2nd number UP makes your estimation SMALLER than the real answer.

? Test the rules out by estimating the answers to these calculations, then calculating the real answers: 28 + 98, 12 × 34, 143 − 55 and 247 ÷ 13. Now, make up your own calculations and check to see if the rules always work.

EXAMPLE: Lukas spent <u>£31.08</u> on sausages in <u>nine days</u>. He thinks that he spent <u>£2.96</u> per day on sausages. Is he correct?

£31.08 rounds <u>down</u> to £30.

9 rounds <u>up</u> to <u>10 days</u>.

30 ÷ 10 = £3 a day

Since the first number was rounded <u>down</u>, and the second number was rounded <u>up</u>, the estimation will be <u>smaller</u> than the real answer.

The real value will be <u>more than £3</u>, so Lukas is <u>wrong</u>.

EXAMPLE:

Catherine plans to drive <u>898 miles</u> during her holiday. Petrol for her car costs <u>17p per mile</u> and she has given herself a petrol budget of <u>£190</u>. Use estimation to work out if she has budgeted enough.

Round 898 to the nearest 100 ➞ 900

Round 17 to the nearest 10 ➞ 20

900 × 20 = 18 000p = £180

898 and 17 were rounded <u>up</u> so your <u>estimation</u> will be <u>bigger than</u> the <u>real</u> value. Since the real value will be <u>less than £180</u>, £190 will be <u>more than enough</u>.

"I can estimate to check the answer of a calculation."

BODMAS

Remember the <u>BODMAS</u> rule for the <u>order</u> to do things in a calculation.

B Brackets **O** **D** Division **M** Multiplication **A** Addition **S** Subtraction

<u>BUT</u> when a calculation only has <u>addition</u> and <u>subtraction</u>,
do it from <u>left</u> to <u>right</u> instead of following BODMAS.

EXAMPLES:
a) $21 - 2 + 3 = 19 + 3 = \underline{22}$
b) $5 \times 4 - 3 + 6 = 20 - 3 + 6 = 17 + 6 = \underline{23}$

Brackets *Can Change the* Answer *to Calculations*

Putting <u>brackets</u> in different places in a calculation can give you <u>different</u> answers.

EXAMPLE: Put <u>one pair of brackets</u> around <u>two numbers</u> in the following calculation to make the answer as <u>large as possible</u>.

$$12 - 8 \times 4 + 20 - 12$$

1) Start by putting <u>brackets</u> round the <u>first</u> pair of numbers.

$(12 - 8) \times 4 + 20 - 12 = 4 \times 4 + 20 - 12$
$= 16 + 20 - 12 = \underline{24}$

Use the rule of BODMAS and don't forget to do addition and subtraction from left to right.

2) Now put <u>brackets</u> round the <u>second</u>, <u>third</u> and <u>fourth</u> pairs of numbers.

$12 - (8 \times 4) + 20 - 12 = 12 - 32 + 20 - 12$
$= -20 + 20 - 12 = \underline{-12}$

$12 - 8 \times (4 + 20) - 12 = 12 - 8 \times 24 - 12$
$= 12 - 192 - 12 = \underline{-192}$

$12 - 8 \times 4 + (20 - 12) = 12 - 8 \times 4 + 8$
$= 12 - 32 + 8 = \underline{-12}$

The largest answer is <u>24</u> with the calculation:
$(12 - 8) \times 4 + 20 - 12$

? Can you get a bigger answer if you put the brackets around more than two numbers? What about if you used more than one pair of brackets?

"I know what order to do things in a calculation."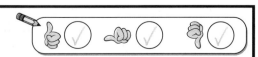

Multiples, Factors and Primes

Using Common Multiples and Common Factors

Common multiples and common factors are multiples and factors
that are shared by two or more numbers.

EXAMPLES:
24 is a common multiple of 8 and 12.
($8 \times 3 = 24$ and $12 \times 2 = 24$)

The common factors of 8 and 12 are 1, 2, 4.
(Factors of 8: 1, 2, 4, 8 and factors of 12: 1, 2, 3, 4, 6, 12)

EXAMPLE: Two toy cars are going round a track. One completes a lap every
12 seconds and one completes a lap every 10 seconds. They begin
on the start line at the same time. How many laps will the cars
have completed the next time they cross the line together?

The first car crosses the line after
12, 24, 36, 48, (60) 72, 84... seconds

The second car crosses the line after
10, 20, 30, 40, 50, (60) 70... seconds

They will next cross the line
together at 60 seconds, after the
first car has completed 5 laps and
the second has completed 6 laps.

? When will they next cross the line together? How many times
will they cross the line together if the race goes on for 100 laps?

Discovering Prime Dates

A prime date is when the day and month are both prime. E.g. 11th July — 11/7.

EXAMPLE: Tom's birthday is on a prime date. There isn't another prime date
within 3 days of his birthday. On what dates could his birthday be?

1. List all the numbers for
   prime months — up to 12.

   2: Feb, 3: March, 5: May, 7: July and 11: Nov

2. Write down all the prime numbers
   for days in a month — up to 31.

   2, 3, 5, 7, 11, 13, 17, 19, 23, 29 and 31

So Tom's birthday could be on:
23 Feb, 23 March, 23 May, 23 July or 23 Nov

23 is the only number listed
that is more than 3 away
from any of the others.

? How many prime dates are there in March? What about in a whole year?

"I know how to find common multiples,
common factors and prime numbers."

Solving Calculation Problems

Break Down Problems Into Steps

EXAMPLE: Kirstie buys <u>170</u> burgers for a BBQ. <u>One fifth</u> of them are veggie burgers. She burns <u>half</u> of the veggie burgers and drops <u>3</u> of the remaining veggie burgers in the mud. How many veggie burgers are left?

STEP 1 Find <u>one fifth</u> of the total number of burgers: $\Longrightarrow$ $170 \div 5 = 34$

STEP 2 She <u>burns half</u>... $\Longrightarrow$ $34 \div 2 = 17$

STEP 3 ... and then <u>drops 3</u>. $\Longrightarrow$ $17 - 3 = \underline{14}$ veggie burgers are left.

EXAMPLE:

Arthur makes and sells robots. <u>Giant</u> robots cost <u>£15</u> to make and he sells them for <u>£25</u>. <u>Super</u> robots cost <u>£18</u> to make and he sells them for <u>£30</u>. One day, he sells <u>5 giant robots</u> and makes a <u>total profit</u> of <u>£98</u>. How many <u>super</u> robots has he sold?

1. First, work out the <u>profit</u> he makes on <u>each robot</u>.

2. Find how much profit he makes from selling <u>5 giant robots</u>.

3. Work out <u>how much</u> of the profit comes from selling <u>super robots</u>.

4. Work out <u>how many</u> super robots make this much profit.

Profit = selling price – cost to make
Giant robot: profit = £25 – £15 = £10
Super robot: profit = £30 – £18 = £12

Profit for 5 giant robots = 5 × £10 = £50

Profit for super robots = £98 – £50 = £48

Number of super robots sold = £48 ÷ £12 = <u>4</u>

? Can you write the working for both of these examples as single sums?

"I can work out what calculations I need to use to solve a problem."

SECTION TWO — CALCULATIONS

Practice Questions

1   Find the missing digits in the calculation on the right.

$$
\begin{array}{r}
2\ 8\ \square\ 5\ 3 \\
\times\qquad\ 3\ \square \\
\hline
\square\ 6\ 9\ 0\ 6 \\
8\ 5\ 3\ \square\ 9\ 0 \\
\hline
\square\ 1\ 0\ 4\ 9\ \square
\end{array}
$$

2   Use the digits 5-9 to make this calculation correct. Each digit can only be used once.

$$
\begin{array}{r}
\square\ \square\ \square\ \square \\
\times\qquad\ \ \square \\
\hline
5\ 4\ 0\ 7\ 2
\end{array}
$$

3   Teo the dog walks 2423 m from his house to the beach.
There is a lamp post every 50 m and the first one is 50 m from his house.

a)   How many lamp posts does Teo pass on his way to the beach?

b)   What is the distance from the last lamp post to the beach?

4   Louis attempts to divided 72 books equally between identical boxes.
He is left with 7 books and each box has more than one book in it.

How many boxes did Louis use?

5   Chris cuts a 456 cm long piece of wood into eight pieces. How long is each piece?

Work it out in your head.

6   Micaela is making a large quantity of chocolate milk. She adds 343 ml of melted chocolate to 6244 ml of milk. She then drinks 452 ml.

How much chocolate milk does she have left? Work it out in your head.

7   98 × 16 = 1568. Which of these gives an estimate closest to the actual value?

100 × 20   100 × 16   98 × 20

Practice Questions

8   Monika's gym membership costs £17.95 a month.
She estimates that in 27 months, she will spend over £600.

     Is Monika correct?

9   Solve the following calculations using BODMAS.

     a) $24 - 2 + 3 \times 4$ b) $39 + 6 \div 2 - 4$ c) $63 + 3 - 8 \times (2 + 4)$

10   Put brackets in the right place in each calculation to make it correct.

     a) $3 + 7 \times 5 - 1 = 31$ b) $16 \div 4 - 2 + 23 = 31$

     c) $24 - 1 + 2 \times 4 = 12$ d) $30 \div 10 \div 5 + 4 = 5$

11   Benjamin is dividing his building blocks into equal piles.
At first he divides them into 20 equal piles, but then he decides
that this is too many and divides them into 8 piles instead.

     Benjamin has less than 100 building blocks.
How many building blocks could he possibly have?

12   Jane says that some years have more prime dates than others.

     Is she correct, and why?

13   Emily buys 120 m of wool. One third of the wool is blue. She uses
half of the blue wool in making a scarf and another 15 m in making a hat.

     How much blue wool does Emily have left once she has finished knitting?

14   374 people bought advance tickets to a festival for £12 each.
126 people bought tickets on the door.
Half of these paid £15 each and the rest paid £20 each for VIP tickets.

     How much money was paid in total for tickets?

Simplifying Fractions

Finding Equivalent Fractions

The <u>numerators</u> and <u>denominators</u> of <u>equivalent</u> fractions can form <u>patterns</u>, e.g.

$$\frac{3}{8} = \frac{6}{16} = \frac{9}{24} = \frac{12}{32} = \frac{15}{40}$$

← The numerators are <u>multiples of 3</u>.
← The denominators are <u>multiples of 8</u>.

EXAMPLE: Find all the fractions with denominators <u>less than 100</u> that are equivalent to $\frac{8}{22}$.

1) <u>Simplify</u> the fraction: $\frac{8}{22} \underset{\div 2}{\overset{\div 2}{\rightleftarrows}} \frac{4}{11}$

? What happens if you don't simplify the fraction first?

2) Write out all the <u>multiples of 11</u> that are <u>less than 100</u> — these will be the <u>denominators</u>.

11, 22, 33, 44, 55, 66, 77, 88, 99

3) The <u>numerators</u> will be the <u>multiples of 4</u>.

$$\frac{4}{11}, \frac{8}{22}, \frac{12}{33}, \frac{16}{44}, \frac{20}{55}, \frac{24}{66}, \frac{28}{77}, \frac{32}{88}, \frac{36}{99}$$

Cross Multiply to Check for Equivalent Fractions

You can check if two fractions are <u>equivalent</u> by <u>cross multiplying</u> the numerators with the denominators.

$$\frac{1}{2} \times \frac{2}{4} \begin{array}{l} = 2 \times 2 = 4 \\ = 1 \times 4 = 4 \end{array}$$

If the two answers are <u>equal</u> then the fractions are <u>equivalent</u>.

EXAMPLE: There are <u>39 cows</u> and <u>65 chickens</u> on a farm. <u>24 cows</u> and <u>40 chickens</u> are sleeping. Farmer Giles claims that the <u>same fraction</u> of the cows and chickens are asleep. Is he correct?

$\frac{24}{39}$ of the cows are sleeping and $\frac{40}{65}$ of the chickens are sleeping.

$\frac{24}{39} \times \frac{40}{65}$ $39 \times 40 = 1560$ The two fractions are equivalent
$24 \times 65 = 1560$ and so Farmer Giles is <u>correct</u>.

? Can you explain why the cross multiplying method works?
Can you think of other ways to check if two fractions are equivalent?

"I can simplify fractions. I can write equivalent fractions with the same denominator."

Ordering Fractions

Putting Fractions On a Number Line

You can <u>compare the sizes</u> of fractions by putting them on a <u>number line</u>.

EXAMPLE: Draw an arrow pointing to $\frac{13}{16}$ on the <u>number line</u> below.

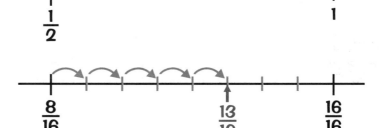

1) Change the numbers on the number line into fractions with a <u>denominator of 16</u>.
$\frac{1}{2} = \frac{8}{16}$ and $1 = \frac{16}{16}$

2) Divide each gap into $16 - 8 = \underline{8 \text{ equal steps}}$. Each step represents $\frac{1}{16}$.

3) Count on <u>5 small steps</u> from $\frac{8}{16}$ to get to $\frac{13}{16}$ and draw an <u>arrow</u>.

? How would you draw an arrow pointing to $\frac{5}{7}$ on the number line above?

EXAMPLE: Which of the fractions $\frac{5}{8}, \frac{7}{9}, \frac{7}{11}$ will appear on the number line on the right?

$\frac{4}{7}$ $\frac{5}{7}$

To lie on the number line, the fraction must be <u>greater than</u> $\frac{4}{7}$ and <u>less than</u> $\frac{5}{7}$. Use <u>equivalent fractions</u> to check.

$\frac{5}{8} = \frac{35}{56}, \frac{4}{7} = \frac{32}{56}$ and $\frac{5}{7} = \frac{40}{56}$ ⟹ $\frac{32}{56} < \frac{35}{56} < \frac{40}{56}$

$\frac{7}{9} = \frac{49}{63}, \frac{4}{7} = \frac{36}{63}$ and $\frac{5}{7} = \frac{45}{63}$ ⟹ $\frac{36}{63} < \frac{45}{63} < \frac{49}{63}$ ← $\frac{7}{9}$ is greater than $\frac{5}{7}$ so won't appear on this number line.

$\frac{7}{11} = \frac{49}{77}, \frac{4}{7} = \frac{44}{77}$ and $\frac{5}{7} = \frac{55}{77}$ ⟹ $\frac{44}{77} < \frac{49}{77} < \frac{55}{77}$

So $\frac{5}{8}$ and $\frac{7}{11}$ lie between $\frac{4}{7}$ and $\frac{5}{7}$ on the number line.

? Can you find other fractions that will fit on this number line?

"I can compare and order fractions, including fractions greater than 1."

Adding and Subtracting Fractions

Adding and Subtracting Mixed Numbers

Before <u>adding</u> and <u>subtracting</u> fractions you should always
make sure that they have the <u>same denominators</u>.
There are <u>different ways</u> that you can add and subtract <u>mixed numbers</u> though.

EXAMPLE: Mika, Jess and Niamh have beetroot juice and cabbage juice shown in these <u>one litre glasses</u>. How much juice do they have in total?

There are $2\frac{2}{3}$ litres of beetroot juice and $1\frac{3}{4}$ litres of cabbage juice.

Mika's method:

1. Change the <u>mixed numbers</u> to <u>improper fractions</u>.

2. Put the fractions over a <u>common denominator</u> and add them together.

$$2\frac{2}{3} + 1\frac{3}{4} = \frac{8}{3} + \frac{7}{4}$$

$$= \frac{32}{12} + \frac{21}{12} = \frac{53}{12} = 4\frac{5}{12} \text{ litres}$$

Jess's method:

1. Add the <u>whole number</u> parts and the <u>fraction parts</u> separately.

2. Put the fractions over a <u>common denominator</u> and add them together.

3. Add the <u>fraction</u> to the <u>whole number</u>.

$$2\frac{2}{3} + 1\frac{3}{4} = 2 + 1 + \frac{2}{3} + \frac{3}{4}$$

$$= 3 + \frac{8}{12} + \frac{9}{12} = 3 + \frac{17}{12}$$

$$= 3 + 1\frac{5}{12} = 4\frac{5}{12} \text{ litres}$$

Niamh's method:

<u>Split</u> the glasses that aren't full into <u>12</u> then combine them into as many <u>full glasses</u> as possible.

So there are $4\frac{5}{12}$ litres.

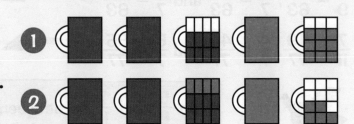

? What do you think are the advantages and disadvantages of each method?

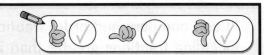

"I can add and subtract fractions by using a common denominator."

Multiplying Fractions

Finding a Fraction of an Unknown Amount

Remember that to multiply two fractions together, you need to multiply the numerators and denominators separately, then simplify your answer.

You can multiply fractions to find proportions of something, even when you don't know the total.

EXAMPLE:

Cheng gives $\frac{1}{4}$ of a cheesecake to his parents to share.
His mum eats $\frac{4}{9}$ and his dad eats $\frac{5}{9}$ of their portion.
What fraction of the whole cheesecake do each of his parents eat?

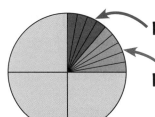

His mum eats $\frac{4}{9}$ of $\frac{1}{4}$. → $\frac{4}{9} \times \frac{1}{4} = \frac{4}{36} = \frac{1}{9}$

'of' just means multiply.

His dad eats $\frac{5}{9}$ of $\frac{1}{4}$. → $\frac{5}{9} \times \frac{1}{4} = \frac{5}{36}$

His mum eats $\frac{1}{9}$ and his dad eats $\frac{5}{36}$ of the whole cheesecake.

EXAMPLE: What fraction of this hexagon is blue?

Each big triangle is $\frac{1}{6}$ of the hexagon.

Each small triangle is $\frac{1}{4}$ of a big triangle.

So each small triangle is $\frac{1}{6} \times \frac{1}{4} = \frac{1}{24}$ of the hexagon.

9 small triangles are blue so $\frac{1}{24} \times 9 = \frac{9}{24} = \frac{3}{8}$ of the hexagon is blue.

 Can you think of other ways to answer the two examples on this page? Can you solve them by dividing fractions by whole numbers?

"I can multiply fractions by other fractions."

Dividing Fractions by Whole Numbers

Dividing <u>fractions</u> by <u>whole numbers</u> isn't too tricky — just <u>multiply</u> the <u>denominator</u> by the <u>whole number</u>. Change <u>mixed numbers</u> to <u>improper fractions</u> before dividing them by whole numbers.

$$\frac{7}{9} \div 8 = \frac{7}{72} \qquad \frac{15}{4} \div 7 = \frac{15}{28} \qquad 3\frac{5}{6} \div 4 = \frac{23}{6} \div 4 = \frac{23}{24}$$

$9 \times 8 \qquad\qquad 4 \times 7 \qquad\qquad 6 \times 4$

Dividing Fractions to find the Best Deal

EXAMPLE:

Jenny hates running but loves maths. Her PE teacher says that Jenny can either run $\frac{3}{4}$ miles by herself or run a total of $3\frac{1}{3}$ miles between her and three friends (they all have to run the same distance). Which option should Jenny choose if she wants to run the shortest distance?

If Jenny <u>splits the run</u> with her friends, she will have to run $3\frac{1}{3} \div 4 = \frac{10}{3} \div 4 = \frac{10}{12}$ miles.

If Jenny <u>runs alone</u> she will have to run $\frac{3}{4} = \frac{9}{12}$ miles.

$\frac{9}{12} < \frac{10}{12}$ so Jenny should run $\frac{3}{4}$ miles by herself.

EXAMPLE:

Cal has just won a game show but has one decision left to make. He can either get $\frac{5}{8}$ of the jackpot and share it equally with two other contestants or $\frac{11}{12}$ of the jackpot and share it equally with three other contestants. Which option will give Cal the most money?

The first option will give Cal $\frac{5}{8} \div 3 = \frac{5}{24} = \frac{10}{48}$ of the jackpot.

The second option will give Cal $\frac{11}{12} \div 4 = \frac{11}{48}$ of the jackpot.

$\frac{10}{48} < \frac{11}{48}$ so the <u>second option</u> gives Cal the most money.

? What would the fractions of the jackpot need to be for Cal to get the same amount of money for either option?

"I can divide fractions by whole numbers."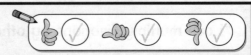

Multiplying or Dividing by 10, 100 or 1000

Remember that to <u>multiply</u> or <u>divide by ten</u>, you just move
all the digits <u>one place value column</u> to the <u>left</u> or <u>right</u>.

4 hundredths becomes 4 tenths

$$1\,8\,.\,6\,4\,7 \times 10 = 1\,8\,6\,.\,4\,7$$

8 units becomes 8 tens

9 tenths becomes 9 hundredths

$$7\,.\,9\,2 \div 10 = 0\,.\,7\,9\,2$$

7 units becomes 7 tenths

× and ÷ by 100 is the Same as × and ÷ by 10 Twice

As long as you can <u>multiply numbers by 10</u> you can also <u>multiply them by 100</u>,
<u>1000</u>, etc. Just multiply by 10 <u>over and over again</u>.

> $100 = 10 \times 10$ so to multiply
> or divide by 100 you multiply
> or divide by <u>10 twice</u> —
> move the digits <u>two places</u>.

> $1000 = 10 \times 10 \times 10$ so to
> multiply or divide by 1000 you
> multiply or divide by <u>10 three times</u>
> — move the digits <u>three places</u>.

? How would you multiply or divide a number by 10 000, 100 000 or 1 000 000?

EXAMPLE: Jess sells jars of jam on her market stall. Each jar contains <u>178 g of jam</u>.
She puts her jars in <u>10 rows</u>. Each row is <u>10 jars long</u> and <u>10 jars high</u>.
How many grams of jam does she have on her market stall?

Jess has $10 \times 10 \times 10$ jars of jam.
Each jar has **178 g** of jam in.

$178 \times 10 \times 10 \times 10 = 178 \times 1000 = 178\,000$

> So she has 178 000 g of
> jam on her market stall.

EXAMPLE: The width of a ping pong ball is approximately
<u>100 000 000 times smaller</u> than the width of the moon.
The moon is about 3500 km wide. How wide is a ping pong ball?

$100\,000\,000 = 10 \times 10 \times 10 \times 10 \times 10 \times 10 \times 10 \times 10$ ← 8 times (notice
there are 8 zeros
in 100 000 000)

You need to divide <u>3500</u> by <u>100 000 000</u> — this is the same as
dividing by 10 <u>eight times</u>. So move all digits <u>8 places</u> to the <u>right</u>.

$3500 \div 100\,000\,000 = 0.00003500 = \underline{0.000035}$ km

? Can you convert this answer so that the units are more appropriate?

"I can multiply or divide numbers by 10, 100 or 1000."

Multiplying and Dividing with Decimals

Keep Track of the Decimal Point

The key thing when multiplying and dividing decimals is to keep track of that pesky little decimal point. It's always a good idea to do an estimation to check that it's in the right place.

EXAMPLES: Put in the decimal point to make these multiplications correct.

Estimate the answer. Then put the decimal point in the place that makes the answer as close as possible to your estimate.

So put the decimal point here to make the answer close to 130.

1) 13.24 × 12 = 15888 → Estimation: 13 × 10 = 130 → 13.24 × 12 = 158.88

2) 8.643 × 38 = 328434 → Estimation: 10 × 40 = 400 → 8.643 × 38 = 328.434

3) 3.24 × 12.23 = 396252 → Estimation: 3 × 10 = 30 → 3.24 × 12.23 = 39.6252

Can you see any link between the number of decimal places in the question and the number of decimal places in the answer? Can you find an example where this doesn't work?

EXAMPLES: Put in the decimal point to make these divisions correct.

1) 64.7 ÷ 4 = 16175
Estimation: 60 ÷ 4 = 15
64.7 ÷ 4 = 16.175

2) 9.678 ÷ 5 = 19356
Estimation: 10 ÷ 5 = 2
9.678 ÷ 5 = 1.9356

3) 978.74 ÷ 25 = 391496
Estimation: 1000 ÷ 25 = 40
978.74 ÷ 25 = 39.1496

4) 78.785 ÷ 20 = 393925
Estimation: 80 ÷ 20 = 4
78.785 ÷ 20 = 3.93925

In these calculations, the number of decimal places in the answer is more than the number of decimal places in the question. Is this always the case when dividing?

"I can multiply and divide decimal numbers by whole numbers."

Rounding Decimals

Different Decimals can Round to the Same Number

Just like when you're <u>rounding whole numbers</u>, lots of decimals round to the <u>same number</u> to a given number of <u>decimal places</u>.

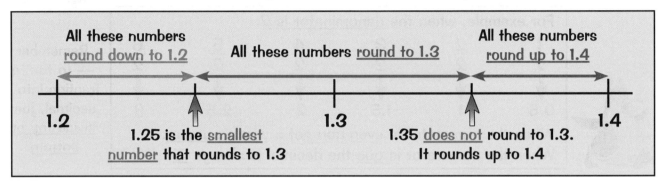

All these numbers <u>round down to 1.2</u>

All these numbers <u>round to 1.3</u>

All these numbers <u>round up to 1.4</u>

1.2

1.25 is the <u>smallest</u> <u>number</u> that rounds to 1.3

1.3

1.35 <u>does not</u> round to 1.3. It rounds up to 1.4

1.4

? What is the biggest number you can find that rounds to 1.3 to one decimal place?

EXAMPLE:

The times in a 100 m race are recorded in seconds to <u>three decimal places</u>. Usain says, "I ran <u>9.8 seconds</u> to one decimal place and <u>9.85 seconds</u> to two decimal places." Write down all of the possible recorded times that Usain could have run.

1. Start by finding all the numbers with <u>three decimal places</u> that round to <u>9.85 to two decimal places</u>.

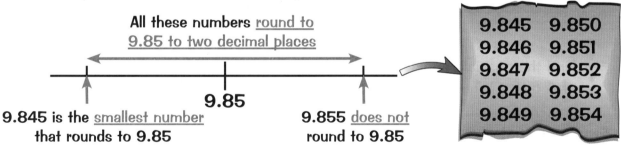

All these numbers <u>round to</u> <u>9.85 to two decimal places</u>

9.85

9.845 is the <u>smallest number</u> that rounds to 9.85

9.855 <u>does not</u> round to 9.85

9.845	9.850
9.846	9.851
9.847	9.852
9.848	9.853
9.849	9.854

2. Check which of these times round to <u>9.8 to one decimal place</u>.

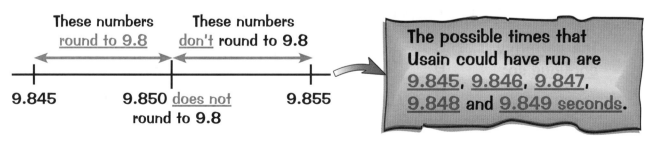

These numbers <u>round to 9.8</u>

These numbers <u>don't</u> round to 9.8

9.845

9.850 <u>does not</u> round to 9.8

9.855

The possible times that Usain could have run are <u>9.845, 9.846, 9.847, 9.848</u> and <u>9.849 seconds</u>.

"I can round decimal numbers to a given number of decimal places."

Converting Fractions to Decimals

Fractions and Decimals Form Patterns

When you convert fractions with the <u>same denominator</u> into <u>decimals</u> they can form <u>patterns</u>.

For example, when the <u>denominator is 2</u>:

$$\frac{1}{2} \qquad \frac{2}{2} \qquad \frac{3}{2} \qquad \frac{4}{2} \qquad \frac{5}{2} \qquad \frac{6}{2}$$

↓ ↓ ↓ ↓ ↓ ↓

0.5   1   1.5   2   2.5   3

When the numerator is <u>even</u> you get a <u>whole number</u>.
When the numerator is <u>odd</u> the decimal is always <u>.5</u>

Remember — to turn a fraction into a decimal, just <u>divide top by bottom</u>.

EXAMPLE: If a fraction with a denominator of 5 is converted to a decimal, what are the possible endings for the decimal?

1. Convert $\frac{1}{5}$, $\frac{2}{5}$, $\frac{3}{5}$, $\frac{4}{5}$ and $\frac{5}{5}$ to decimals.

$$\frac{1}{5} = 0.\underline{2} \qquad \frac{2}{5} = 0.\underline{4} \qquad \frac{3}{5} = 0.\underline{6} \qquad \frac{4}{5} = 0.\underline{8} \qquad \frac{5}{5} = 1$$

2. After this, the part <u>after the decimal point</u> will repeat in the <u>same order</u>.

$$\frac{6}{5} = 1.\underline{2} \qquad \frac{7}{5} = 1.\underline{4} \qquad \frac{8}{5} = 1.\underline{6} \qquad \frac{9}{5} = 1.\underline{8} \qquad \frac{10}{5} = 2$$

So the only possible endings are <u>.2</u>, <u>.4</u>, <u>.6</u>, <u>.8</u> or a <u>whole number</u>.

? Find the possible endings for the decimals when the fraction has a denominator of 4 or 8. What do you notice about the number of different decimal endings?

Fractions that give <u>recurring decimals</u> can also form interesting patterns.

EXAMPLE: $\frac{1}{9} = 0.1111...$ and $\frac{2}{9} = 0.2222...$

Without using a calculator, find the values of $\frac{5}{9}$ and $\frac{8}{9}$.

The <u>pattern</u> will <u>continue</u> so:

$$\frac{3}{9} = 0.3333..., \quad \frac{4}{9} = 0.4444..., \quad \frac{5}{9} = 0.5555...,$$

$$\frac{6}{9} = 0.6666..., \quad \frac{7}{9} = 0.7777...., \quad \frac{8}{9} = 0.8888...$$

"I can convert fractions to decimals by dividing."

Fractions, Decimals and Percentages

Using Fractions, Decimals and Percentages...

Fractions, decimals and percentages are three different ways of writing a number. The different forms are each useful in different situations:

FRACTIONS can be used to show an amount or to show a proportion.

For example, Joan has walked $2\frac{2}{3}$ miles or eaten $\frac{1}{4}$ of a cake.

DECIMALS are best used to show amounts. They have an advantage over fractions as they are easier to compare and order.

E.g. it's difficult to say which of $\frac{213}{50}$ kg and $\frac{534}{125}$ kg is bigger,

but as decimals (4.26 kg and 4.272 kg) it's easy to compare them.

PERCENTAGES are only used to show a proportion of an amount. For example, a supermarket increased the price of its lemons by 25%, or 50% of badgers are pure evil. They are also easier to compare and order than fractions.

EXAMPLES: Convert the numbers in these sentences into their most useful form.

1. A water park is offering tickets at 0.6 of the original price. This is still more than the local pool which costs £$2\frac{2}{5}$.

Decimals aren't great for showing proportions, so change 0.6 to a percentage or fraction. ⟶ $0.6 = 60\% = \frac{3}{5}$

Although fractions can show amounts, decimals given to two decimal places are more useful for money. ⟶ £$2\frac{2}{5}$ = **£2.40**

2. The sales of caterpillar repellent increased by $\frac{8}{25}$ last year. This year they increased by $\frac{7}{20}$.

The fractions would be more useful as percentages — then you could see which year had the greater increase.

$\frac{8}{25} = \frac{32}{100} = \underline{32\%}$

$\frac{7}{20} = \frac{35}{100} = \underline{35\%}$

"I can convert between fractions, decimals and percentages."

Practice Questions

1. A box has less than 50 chocolates in it.
    Linda takes $\frac{2}{13}$ of the chocolates from a box.

    How many chocolates could Linda have taken?

2. Which of these pairs of fractions are equivalent?

    $\frac{2}{7}$ and $\frac{12}{49}$ $\frac{3}{9}$ and $\frac{11}{33}$ $\frac{7}{11}$ and $\frac{77}{110}$ $\frac{15}{24}$ and $\frac{35}{56}$

3. As accurately as possible, draw arrows pointing to $\frac{5}{12}$ and $\frac{5}{6}$ on this number line.

    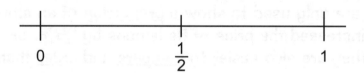

4. Michelle is writing a project on the Vikings. The project must be less than 8 pages long. She has written $3\frac{2}{3}$ pages about their home life, $2\frac{2}{5}$ pages about their battles and $1\frac{5}{6}$ pages about their weapons.

    Is Michelle's project too long?

5. Stan gets some pocket money. He spends $\frac{1}{4}$ on comic books and then spends $\frac{7}{9}$ of what is left on sweets.

    What fraction of his pocket money did he spend on sweets?

6. Alice has a pile of sand that she is going to use to build a sandcastle.
    Will there be more sand in each castle wall if she takes $\frac{3}{5}$ of the pile and builds 8 identical walls, or if or she takes $\frac{7}{8}$ of the pile and builds 10 identical walls?

Practice Questions

7 Draw lines to match the calculations below that will give the same answer.

3.5 × 10 × 10 × 10

0.0035 × 100   350 ÷ 1000

0.35 × 10 × 10   35 × 100

35 000 ÷ 10 ÷ 10 ÷ 10

8 Use estimation to decide if each of these statements could be true, or is definitely false.

  a) If I share 11.52 kg of carrots equally between 12 people, then each person will get 0.96 kg.

  b) When 58 pipes, each with a length of 3.24 m, are joined end-to-end, the total length is 1624.23 m.

9 A stopwatch measures time in seconds to two decimal places. John attempts to break the school record for eating a peanut butter and jam sandwich in the fastest time. The current school record is 9.623 seconds.

  John's stopwatch shows that he ate the sandwich in 9.62 seconds. Has he definitely broken the school record?

10 $\frac{1}{11} = 0.090909...$, $\frac{2}{11} = 0.181818...$ and $\frac{3}{11} = 0.272727...$

  Without using a calculator, find the values of $\frac{4}{11}$, $\frac{5}{11}$ and $\frac{6}{11}$.

11 Convert the numbers in the sentence below into their most useful form.

  My best friend said that in 2.25 hours the local clothing shop is selling all of its sweaters for £$5\frac{3}{20}$ each.

Relative Sizes

Scaling up and down is just about <u>multiplying</u> and <u>dividing</u>.

Use Scaling to Change Amounts Up or Down

EXAMPLE:

Part of a recipe is shown. The recipe makes <u>6 cakes</u>.

How much of each ingredient is needed to make <u>9 cakes</u>?

> 450 g Flour
> 120 g Sugar
> 240 ml Milk

1. First, you need to <u>divide by 6</u> to find out how much of each ingredient you would need for <u>1 cake</u>:

> 450 g ÷ 6 = 75 g Flour
> 120 g ÷ 6 = 20 g Sugar
> 240 ml ÷ 6 = 40 ml Milk

2. Then you need to <u>multiply by 9</u> to find out how much of each ingredient you need for <u>9 cakes</u>:

> 75 g × 9 = <u>675 g</u> Flour
> 20 g × 9 = <u>180 g</u> Sugar
> 40 ml × 9 = <u>360 ml</u> Milk

? Can you find a quicker way of scaling up the recipe from 6 cakes to 9 cakes by multiplying by a single number?

EXAMPLE:

Paul is making a cake using the recipe above. He only has <u>200 ml of milk</u> in his fridge. How much of the other ingredients does he need if he uses <u>all</u> of the milk?

1. Find how much milk he <u>has</u> compared to how much the recipe says he <u>needs</u>:

$$200 \text{ ml} \div 240 \text{ ml} = \frac{200}{240} = \frac{5}{6}$$

2. Then multiply this fraction by the amounts of <u>flour</u> and <u>sugar</u> given in the recipe:

<u>Flour:</u>
$$\frac{5}{6} \times 450 \text{ g} = \underline{375 \text{ g}}$$

<u>Sugar:</u>
$$\frac{5}{6} \times 120 \text{ g} = \underline{100 \text{ g}}$$

? What is the maximum number of cakes that can be made using 2.5 kg of flour, 0.7 kg of sugar and 1.5 litres of milk?

"I can solve problems that are to do with the relative sizes of two amounts."

Relative Sizes

Maps show Scaled Down Distances

Maps show <u>real-life distances</u> on a <u>drawing</u>. They use a <u>scale</u> to tell you how much you need to <u>scale up</u> to find the real-life distance.

> 1 cm to 30 m means "for every 1 cm on the map, there are 30 m in real life."
> 1 cm = 2 km means "for every 1 cm on the map, there are 2 km in real life."

EXAMPLE:

Cliff finds the treasure map shown below. The map also comes with a set of instructions. <u>Mark with a cross</u> the place where the treasure is buried.

If standing at Skull Rock you be, then 'tis 40 m to the palm tree.

Take a walk from the wreck to the sandy ground. After 30 m, there's treasure to be found.

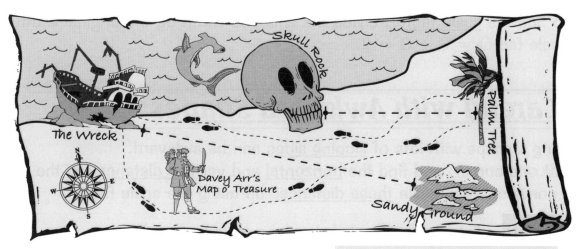

1. On the map, the distance from Skull Rock to the palm tree is <u>4 cm</u>.

   Scale: 4 cm = 40 m
   So 1 cm = 40 ÷ 4 = 10 m

   This means that for every <u>1 cm on the map</u>, there are <u>10 m in real life</u>.

2. The treasure is <u>30 m</u> from the wreck in real life:

   30 m = 30 ÷ 10 = 3 cm on the map

3. So draw a cross <u>3 cm</u> along the line from the wreck to the sandy ground.

? The treasure map scale can also be written as 1:1000 — why do you think that is?

"I can solve problems that are to do with the relative sizes of two amounts."

Scale Factors

Compare Lengths to find the Scale Factor

You can work out the <u>scale factor</u> of an enlargement by <u>measuring</u> matching lengths in the two shapes and then <u>dividing</u> one by the other.

EXAMPLE: Find the scale factor used to enlarge the car below.

Enlarged to give

Make sure you measure <u>the same bit</u> of the two shapes.

Measure the <u>width</u> of the <u>original</u> car = **3** cm
Measure the <u>width</u> of the <u>enlarged</u> car = **6** cm

To find the <u>scale factor</u>, divide the enlarged width by the original width:
Scale factor = 6 ÷ 3 = <u>**2**</u>.

Be Careful with Awkward Shapes

Enlarging a shape with lots of <u>sloping sides</u> can be awkward.
Start at one corner, and find the <u>horizontal</u> and <u>vertical distances</u> to the other corners. Then scale <u>those distances</u> up using the scale factor.

EXAMPLE: Enlarge the triangle below by a scale factor of <u>2</u>.

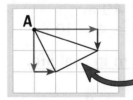

Starting at <u>corner A</u>, the other two corners are:

3 units right and 1 unit down,
1 unit right and 2 units down.

Pick any point to be the new corner A (call it A').

<u>Multiply</u> these distances by the <u>scale factor</u> (2).
Starting at A', the new corners are:

3 × 2 = 6 units right and 1 × 2 = 2 units down,
1 × 2 = 2 units right and 2 × 2 = 4 units down.

Join the corners to give the enlarged triangle.

? Try enlarging some of your own shapes using different scale factors. Can you see a pattern in how the number of squares inside the shape changes when you enlarge it?

"I can enlarge a shape by a scale factor and I can find the scale factor of an enlarged shape."

Percentages of Amounts

Divide to find Percentages of Amounts

Finding percentages of amounts is <u>easy</u> if you know what to <u>divide by</u>:

$$25\% = \frac{25}{100} = \frac{1}{4}$$

So to <u>find 25% of something</u>, just <u>divide it by 4</u>.

$$1\% = \frac{1}{100}$$

So to <u>find 1% of something</u>, just <u>divide it by 100</u>.

EXAMPLE: Sabine started with <u>200</u> pebbles in her collection.
- She <u>gave away 4%</u> of the pebbles to some friends.
- Her Dad then <u>added 25%</u> to her collection.
- She then <u>lost 15%</u> of her pebbles in a tragic accident.

Did her collection get bigger or smaller overall? By how much?

1 Start by finding <u>4% of 200</u>:   1% of 200 = 200 ÷ 100 = 2
So 4% of 200 = 2 × 4 = 8

So Sabine has 200 − 8 = 192 pebbles after she has given 4% away.

2 Now find <u>25% of 192</u>:   25% of 192 = 192 ÷ 4 = 48

She now has 192 + 48 = 240 pebbles after her Dad adds to her collection.

3 Next, find <u>15% of 240</u>:   10% of 240 = 240 ÷ 10 = 24
5% of 240 = 24 ÷ 2 = 12
So 15% of 240 = 24 + 12 = 36

So she's left with 240 − 36 = 204 pebbles.
She started with 200, so overall her collection gets <u>bigger</u> by <u>4 pebbles</u>.

? Sabine says "−4% + 25% − 15% = 6%, so my collection has changed by 6% overall." Is she correct? Can you explain why/why not?

EXAMPLE: Sabine is offered <u>46% of 700</u> pebbles or <u>80% of 400</u> pebbles to add to her collection. Which should she take?

1 46% = 50% − 4%
50% of 700 = 700 ÷ 2 = 350
1% of 700 = 700 ÷ 100 = 7
4% of 700 = 7 × 4 = 28
So <u>46% of 700</u> = 350 − 28 = <u>322</u>

2 10% of 400 = 400 ÷ 10 = 40,
so <u>80% of 400</u> = 40 × 8 = <u>320</u>

To get the most pebbles, Sabine should take <u>46% of 700</u>.

"I can find a percentage of an amount."

Comparing Using Percentages

Use Fractions to find Percentage Amounts

To write one number as a percentage of another, first write the two numbers as a fraction, and then find an equivalent fraction with a denominator of 100.

EXAMPLE:

A class is doing a science experiment. They have to make a mixture which is 65% water, 30% acid and 5% dye. The table below shows the amounts of each ingredient that some people in the class used. Who got the mixture right?

	Water (ml)	Acid (ml)	Dye (ml)
Mo	260	100	40
Jess	120	60	20
Mikael	195	90	15

1 First, find the total amount of mixture that each of them made:

→ 260 + 100 + 40 = **400 ml**
→ 120 + 60 + 20 = **200 ml**
→ 195 + 90 + 15 = **300 ml**

2 For each person, work out the percentage of the total that the ingredients make up:

Mo

$$\% \text{ water} = \frac{260}{400} = \frac{65}{100} = \underline{65\%} \quad (\div 4) \quad ✓$$

$$\% \text{ acid} = \frac{100}{400} = \frac{25}{100} = \underline{25\%} \quad (\div 4) \quad ✗$$

Jess

$$\% \text{ water} = \frac{120}{200} = \frac{60}{100} = \underline{60\%} \quad (\div 2) \quad ✗$$

> The percentage of one ingredient in the mixture is wrong, so the mixture can't be right.

Mikael

$$\% \text{ water} = \frac{195}{300} = \frac{65}{100} = \underline{65\%} \quad (\div 3) \quad ✓$$

$$\% \text{ acid} = \frac{90}{300} = \frac{30}{100} = \underline{30\%} \quad (\div 3) \quad ✓$$

$$\% \text{ dye} = \frac{15}{300} = \frac{5}{100} = \underline{5\%} \quad (\div 3) \quad ✓$$

So Mikael is the only one who got the mixture right.

? Try to work out some other combinations of ingredients which make the correct mixture. What do you notice about the amounts of each ingredient?

"I can use percentages to compare amounts."

Unequal Sharing

EXAMPLE: 3 friends helped a farmer find some lost sheep.

For every sheep that Ashid found, Beth found <u>3 sheep</u>.
For every sheep that Beth found, Carol found <u>2 sheep</u>.

The friends found <u>150</u> sheep in total. How many sheep did they <u>each find</u>?

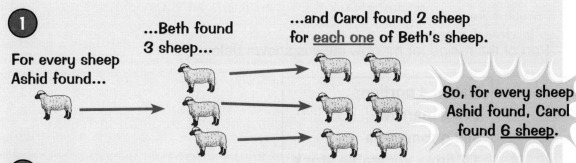

1 For every sheep Ashid found... ...Beth found 3 sheep... ...and Carol found 2 sheep for <u>each one</u> of Beth's sheep.

So, for every sheep Ashid found, Carol found <u>6 sheep</u>.

2 There are 1 + 3 + 6 = <u>10</u> shares in total.
Ashid found 1 share, Beth found 3 shares and Carol found 6 shares.

3 Divide 150 by 10 to find the amount for <u>ONE SHARE</u>,
then multiply to find the number each person found.

So... 150 ÷ 10 = 15 (for 1 share)
15 × 3 = 45 (for 3 shares)
15 × 6 = 90 (for 6 shares)

> Ashid found <u>15 sheep</u>
> Beth found <u>45 sheep</u>
> Carol found <u>90 sheep</u>

EXAMPLE: Ashid found his sheep in <u>2 hours</u>, Beth took <u>4 hours</u> and Carol took <u>6 hours</u> to find all her sheep.

The farmer pays the three friends <u>£240</u> to share between them.
Is it better for <u>Beth</u> if they split the money in the <u>proportion</u> of <u>time spent looking</u> or <u>sheep found</u>?

They spent a total of 2 + 4 + 6 = 12 hours looking for the sheep.
If they split the money in the proportion of <u>time spent looking</u>:
£240 ÷ 12 = £20 (for 1 hour), so Beth would get £20 × 4 = <u>£80</u> (for 4 hours)

If they split in the proportion of <u>sheep found</u>: £240 ÷ 10 = £24 (for one share)
So Beth would get £24 × 3 = <u>£72</u> (for 3 shares)

So it's better for Beth if they split the money in the proportion of <u>time spent looking</u>.

? If the amount the farmer pays the friends changed, would it change the answer?

"I can work out how to share things unequally."

34

1   Toby bought 6 pairs of socks for £12.60.

He liked them so much that he went back to the same shop the next day.
How many pairs of the same socks can he buy with £21?

2   Part of the recipe for marrow stew is shown below.

> **Makes 4 portions:**
> **800 g marrow**
> **500 g tomatoes**
> **1.2 litres vegetable stock**
> **250 g mushrooms**

a)   Ruth has 2400 g of marrows. How many portions can she make?

b)   What amounts of the other ingredients does she need?

3   Chelsea is building a model aeroplane.
The model has a wingspan of 50 cm and is 57 cm long.

She knows that the wingspan of the real plane is 35 m.
What is the length of the real plane?

4   Shape A is enlarged to give shape B.

a)   Work out the scale factor used
in the enlargement.

b)   Enlarge shape A by a scale
factor of 2. Label your shape C.

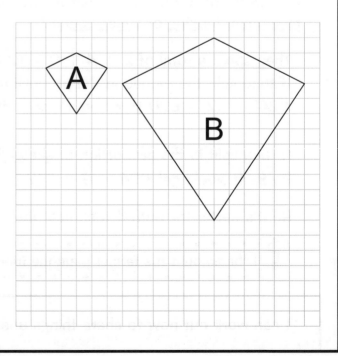

Practice Questions

5   Tom wants to buy a waterproof coat.

He sees a green coat which is 57% of its original price of £300.
He also sees an orange coat which is 75% of its original price of £160.

Which coat do you think he should buy? Why?

6   Taylor is trying to find out how many people are going to a school disco.

She asks everyone in Years 5 and 6 whether they are going.
The table shows the answers she gets.

	Yes	No	Maybe
Year 5	32	23	9
Year 6	29	4	17

Taylor says "The disco is more popular in Year 5 because more pupils said yes."
Explain using percentages why she is incorrect.

7   3 friends are sharing out 90 football stickers.

For every 2 stickers Shaun gives to Ben, he keeps 3 for himself.
Adam gets half as many stickers as Ben.

How many more stickers than Adam does Shaun get?

8   Jules is making a fruit juice cocktail.

He uses 3 parts pineapple juice for every 2 parts apple juice.
He uses twice as much orange juice as apple juice.
He makes 270 ml of the cocktail in total.

How much pineapple juice does he use?

Sequences

Decimal and Fraction Sequences

Look at this <u>number sequence</u>:   2.5, 4.0, 5.5, 7.0, 8.5...

The <u>rule</u> is: <u>Add on 1.5</u> to get from one term to the next.

EXAMPLE: A number sequence goes $9, 8\frac{1}{2}, 8, 7\frac{1}{2}, 7...$

1 What is the rule to get from one term to the next?

$9 - 8\frac{1}{2} = \frac{1}{2}$
so the rule is: SUBTRACT $\frac{1}{2}$

2 What is the 8th number in the sequence?

Carry on the sequence by subtracting $\frac{1}{2}$:
$9, 8\frac{1}{2}, 8, 7\frac{1}{2}, 7, 6\frac{1}{2}, 6, \boxed{5\frac{1}{2}}...$
$5\frac{1}{2}$ is the 8th number in the sequence.

? Which position will have the first negative term?

Other Types of Sequences

Once you know the rule for a sequence, you can <u>follow</u> it and <u>continue</u> the sequence forever, and ever, and ever, and ever, and ever, and ever, and ever, and ever...

EXAMPLE: Find the <u>rule</u> for the sequence 1, 2, 4, 7, 11... then continue the sequence for the next <u>two</u> terms.

Find the <u>differences</u> <u>between terms</u>.

1 → 2 → 4 → 7 → 11
  + 1   + 2   + 3   + 4

The differences between terms are <u>different</u> each time, so look for a <u>pattern</u> between the <u>differences</u>.

The differences increase by one each time so the rule is "<u>add one more than you did to the last number.</u>"

So the next two terms are:
11 + 5 = <u>16</u> and
16 + 6 = <u>22</u>

? Guess how many terms in the sequence will be less than 100, then work it out. How close was your guess?

"I can generate and describe number sequences."

Missing Number Problems

Letters Can Stand For Numbers

You can turn calculations with letters into ones with numbers by substituting.

EXAMPLE: If A = 2, B = 5, C = 7, D = 10 and E = 3 then...

A + B = C	D – E – A = B	2B = D
2 + 5 = 7	10 – 3 – 2 = 5	2 × 5 = 10

A number followed by a letter just means 'multiply'. So 2B = 2 × B.

Fill in these calculations with the correct missing letter:

D + A – C = ☐   10 + 2 – 7 = 12 – 7 = 5.
B = 5, so the missing letter is **B**.

4A – B = ☐   4 × 2 – 5 = 8 – 5 = 3.
E = 3, so the missing letter is **E**.

? Try making all the numbers from 1 to 20 by adding, subtracting, multiplying or dividing the letters A-E. For example, 1 = E – A. Can you find different ways to make the same number?

You Can Use Letters in Missing Number Puzzles

EXAMPLE: Each letter stands for a number in the grid puzzle below. Find the totals for each row and column.

1 Work out the value of each letter.

X	X	X	6
Y	Z	X	
Z	Y	Z	
	12	10	

X + X + X = 6, so **X = 2**.

Since X = 2, 2 + 2 + Z = 10 so **Z = 6**.

Since X = 2 and Z = 6, 2 + 6 + Y = 12 so **Y = 4**.

2 Then find the totals.

2	2	2	6
4	6	2	12
6	4	6	16
12	12	10	

"I can solve missing number problems using symbols and letters."

Two Missing Numbers

Two Facts for Two Missing Number Problems

EXAMPLE: Max bought X chocolate bars and Y jelly snakes. Chocolate bars weigh <u>40 g</u> and jelly snakes weigh <u>20 g</u>. Max bought <u>4</u> items, with a total weight of <u>120 g</u>. How many of each item did he buy?

Max bought 4 items in total. ⟹ X + Y = 4 ⟸ You need to find values of X and Y that make both these correct.

X chocolate bars will weigh 40X g and Y jelly snakes will weight 20Y g. The total weight was 120 g. ⟹ 40X + 20Y = 120

Write down the pairs of X and Y that add together to make 4. ⟹ 0 and 4, 1 and 3, 2 and 2, 3 and 1, 4 and 0.

Put each of these pairs into 40X + 20Y and see if they make 120.

X = 0, Y = 4: 0 + 80 = 80 ✗   X = 1, Y = 3: 40 + 60 = 100 ✗
X = 2, Y = 2: 80 + 40 = 120 ✔   X = 3, Y = 1: 120 + 20 = 140 ✗
X = 4, Y = 0: 160 + 0 = 160 ✗

Max bought <u>2</u> chocolate bars and <u>2</u> jelly snakes.

Some Problems May Have Several Answers

EXAMPLE: Arianna went on <u>four</u> different trains during her holiday.

She spent a total of <u>7 hours</u> on Train A, Train B, Train C and Train D.

- She spent a total of <u>2</u> hours on Trains <u>A</u> and <u>B</u>.
- She spent a total of <u>3</u> hours on Trains <u>B</u> and <u>C</u>.
- She spent a total of <u>5</u> hours on Trains <u>C</u> and <u>D</u>.

How long might Arianna have spent on each train?

1. Try <u>substituting</u> numbers. A + B = 2 hours, so start by trying <u>A = 1</u> and <u>B = 1</u>.
2. If <u>B = 1</u>, then B + C = 3 means that <u>C = 2</u>.
3. So if <u>C = 2</u>, then C + D = 5 means that <u>D = 3</u>.
4. Now check to see if these numbers add up to 7: 1 + 1 + 2 + 3 = 7.
   So one possible answer is: A = 1 hr, B = 1 hr, C = 2 hrs and D = 3 hrs.

? Can you find any other possible answers? (Hint: one train could take half an hour.)

"I can find pairs of numbers to solve problems with two unknowns, and list all possible combinations."

Formulas

You can Write Formulas Using Words or Letters

Formulas can be used to work out <u>one amount</u> when you're given <u>other amounts</u>.

EXAMPLE:

Sammi buys <u>24</u> chocolate eclairs. She eats <u>two eclairs every day</u>.
Write a formula for <u>N</u>, the number of eclairs she'll have left after <u>d</u> days.

1. She starts off with <u>24</u> eclairs.  24

2. She eats <u>2</u> every day. 2 × number of days = 2d

 3. <u>Subtract</u> the number she has eaten from <u>24</u> to find the number she has left.

$$\text{Number of eclairs left} = 24 - \left(2 \times \text{number of days}\right)$$
$$N = 24 - 2d$$

? Why won't the formula work after 12 days?

Use Formulas to Describe Pattern Sequences

EXAMPLE: Which of these <u>formulas</u> describes the number of squares in each pattern of this sequence?

A Number of squares = 4 × pattern number

B Number of squares = 3 × pattern number − 1

C Number of squares = 3 × pattern number + 1

Pattern 1   Pattern 2   Pattern 3

Put each <u>pattern number</u> into each formula to see if it gives the right number of squares.
Pattern 1 has 4 squares, pattern 2 has 7 squares and pattern 3 has 10 squares.

A Number of squares = 4 × pattern number
Pattern 1:   4 × 1 = 4 ✔
Pattern 2:   4 × 2 = 8 ✘ — Pattern 2 should be 7 so this formula isn't correct.

B Number of squares = 3 × pattern number − 1
Pattern 1: 3 × 1 − 1 = 2 ✘
Pattern 1 should be 4 so this formula isn't correct.

? Can you draw your own pattern sequences for each of the incorrect formulas?

C Number of squares = 3 × pattern number + 1
Pattern 1: 3 × 1 + 1 = 4 ✔
Pattern 2: 3 × 2 + 1 = 7 ✔
Pattern 3: 3 × 3 + 1 = 10 ✔

So this is the <u>correct formula</u>.

"I can use formulas written in words."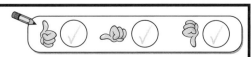

Practice Questions

1   What is the rule to get from one term to the next in the following sequences?

     a)   2, 4.5, 7, 9.5, 12...

     b) $7, 6\frac{3}{4}, 6\frac{1}{2}, 6\frac{1}{4}, 6...$

2   What is the 8th term in each of the following sequences?

     a) $2, 2\frac{3}{4}, 3\frac{1}{2}, 4\frac{1}{4}, 5...$

     b)   11, 7.5, 4, 0.5, –3...

3   The rule for a sequence is "double the previous number and add 1".
     If the first term of the sequence is 2, what are the next five terms?

4   If x = 6, y = 7 and z = 8, find the following:

     a)   x + y

     b)   3z – y

     c)   2x – y + 4z

5   Given that p = 6, r = 5 and s = 3, fill in the blanks
     with letters to make these calculations correct.

     a)   ☐ + ☐ = 11

     b)   4 ☐ – ☐ = 17

     c)   ☐ × ☐ – ☐ = 13

Practice Questions

6   Find the totals for each row and column on this number puzzle grid.

G	H	H	K	12
G	K	K	K	
G	G	H	H	14
G	K	K	H	
16				

7   Tara bought a total of 18 books and games at a car boot sale.
She bought 4 more books (b) than games (g).

How many of each did she buy?

8   Ailsa buys three different pastries from the bakery and spends 90p.

Pastry A is twice the cost of pastry B.
Pastry A and pastry B cost 60p in total.
Pastry B and pastry C cost 50p in total.

How much does each pastry cost?

9   Matilda collects badges. She already has 50,
but gets two more each time she cuts the grass.

Write a formula in words for the number of badges she has at the end of a year.

10   A pattern sequence is shown on the right.

a)   Fill in the box below so that the
formula describes the number
of circles in each pattern:

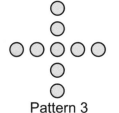

Pattern 1
Pattern 2
Pattern 3

Number of circles = 4 × pattern number − ▢

b)   Use your formula to work out how many
circles there will be in the 30th pattern.

Units

Use Conversion Factors To Solve Problems

These <u>conversion factors</u> tell you how to <u>change</u> between <u>large</u> and <u>small</u> units.

1 <u>kg</u> = 1000 <u>g</u>

1 <u>cm</u> = 10 <u>mm</u>   1 <u>m</u> = 100 <u>cm</u>
1 <u>km</u> = 1000 <u>m</u>

1 <u>litre</u> = 1000 <u>ml</u>

EXAMPLE: A cactus is <u>150 cm</u> tall and grows <u>5 mm</u> each week.
A sunflower is <u>50 cm</u> tall and grows <u>60 mm</u> each week. How
much taller will the cactus be than the sunflower after 8 weeks?

1. Find how much the <u>cactus</u> and <u>sunflower</u> grow each week in <u>cm</u>.	1 cm = 10 mm, so each week: the cactus grows 5 ÷ 10 = 0.5 cm, the sunflower grows 60 ÷ 10 = 6 cm.
2. Work out how tall <u>each plant</u> will be after <u>8 weeks</u>.	0.5 cm × 8 weeks = 4 cm, so the cactus will be 150 + 4 = <u>154 cm</u> tall.
	6 cm × 8 weeks = 48 cm, so the sunflower will be 50 + 48 = <u>98 cm</u> tall.
3. Work out the <u>difference</u> in height between the two.	So the cactus will be 154 cm − 98 cm = <u>56 cm</u> taller.

? How many weeks will it be before the sunflower is taller than the cactus?

EXAMPLE: There are <u>1000 kg</u> in a <u>tonne</u>. Harry sold <u>2.5 tonnes</u>
of sand last year. He sold it in bags of <u>100 g</u>.
<u>How many</u> bags did he sell?

1 Convert 2.5 tonnes into kg: ➤ 1 tonne = 1000 kg,
so 2.5 × 1000 = 2500 kg

2 Convert 2500 kg into g: ➤ 1 kg = 1000 g,
so 2500 × 1000 = 2 500 000 g

3 Divide 2 500 000 g by 100 g. ➤ 2 500 000 ÷ 100
= <u>25 000 bags</u>

"I can convert between units for measurements
of length, mass and volume."

Units

You Can Convert Time in Multiple Steps

> 1 minute = 60 seconds   1 hour = 60 minutes   1 day = 24 hours
>
> 1 week = 7 days   1 year = 365 days or 366 days in a leap year

EXAMPLE: Cat spends <u>4 hours</u> per day nibbling cheese. In a whole <u>leap year</u>, how many <u>days</u> does she spend nibbling cheese?

1 Multiply 4 hours by
1 leap year = 366 days.

4 × 366 = 1464 hours per leap year

2 Convert 1464 hours into days:
1 day = 24 hours

1464 ÷ 24 = <u>61 days</u> in a leap year

? Choose something you do every day — e.g. sleeping, eating, picking fluff out of your belly button. How much of a year do you spend doing it?

Convert Distances to Solve Real-Life Problems

Remember that <u>8 kilometres</u> ≈ <u>5 miles</u>.

> To convert miles to km, ÷ by 5 then × by 8.
>
> To convert km to miles, ÷ by 8 then × by 5.

EXAMPLE: Use the map below to find the <u>shortest</u> route from Ruth's house to the beach.

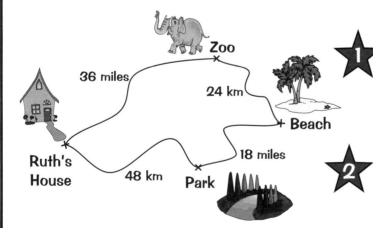

1 Ruth's house to the beach, via the zoo:
36 miles + 24 km
24 km = 24 ÷ 8 × 5 = 15 miles
So it is 36 + 15 = <u>51 miles</u>

2 Ruth's house to the beach, via the park:
48 km + 18 miles
48 km = 48 ÷ 8 × 5 = 30 miles
So it is 30 + 18 = <u>48 miles</u>

? How could you convert kilometres to miles in a single step?
How about miles to kilometres?

So Ruth's shortest route to the beach is <u>48 miles</u>, <u>via the park</u>.

"I can convert between different units of time, and between miles and kilometres."

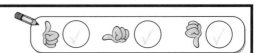

Area of a Triangle

Different Triangles Can Have the Same Area

EXAMPLE: Draw <u>three different</u> triangles below that have the same <u>base</u>, <u>height</u> and <u>area</u> as the one shown.

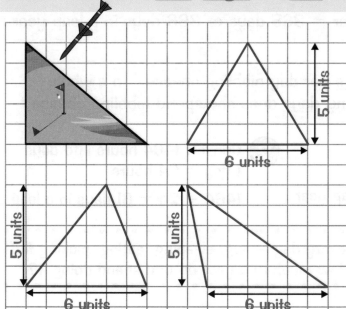

$$\text{Area} = \frac{1}{2} \times \text{base} \times \text{height}$$

The triangle has a height of <u>5 units</u> and a base of <u>6 units</u>. Any other triangle with the same base and height will have the <u>same area</u>.

The area of all these triangles is:

$\frac{1}{2} \times 6 \times 5 = \underline{15 \text{ square units}}$

? Can you draw other triangles with the same area but a different base and height?

EXAMPLE: Draw two different <u>right-angled</u> triangles with an area of <u>4 cm²</u>.

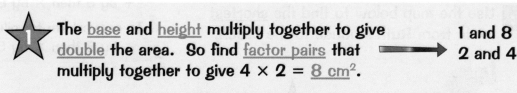

1 The <u>base</u> and <u>height</u> multiply together to give <u>double</u> the area. So find <u>factor pairs</u> that multiply together to give $4 \times 2 = \underline{8 \text{ cm}^2}$.

1 and 8
2 and 4

2 Choose one pair of factors for the <u>base</u> and <u>height</u> and draw a right-angled triangle.

3 Now choose a different pair of factors for the <u>base</u> and <u>height</u>, and draw the triangle.

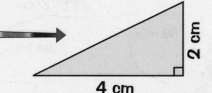

? Are there any other triangles that will work?
Hint: could one have a height of 0.5 cm?

"I can calculate the area of a triangle."

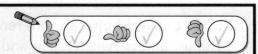

Area of a Parallelogram

Different Parallelograms Can Have the Same Area

The formula for the <u>area of a parallelogram</u> is:

$$\text{Area} = \text{base} \times \text{height}$$

EXAMPLE: Jack is drawing parallelograms which have an area of 12 cm². He starts to record his attempts in the table below. Complete Jack's table.

Base	1 cm	2 cm	3 cm	4 cm	5 cm
Height	12 cm	6 cm			

1 The <u>base</u> and <u>height</u> need to multiply to give <u>12 cm²</u>.
So if the base is <u>3 cm</u>, the height must be 12 ÷ 3 = <u>4 cm</u>,
and if the base is <u>4 cm</u>, the height must be 12 ÷ 4 = <u>3 cm</u>.

2 There is <u>no whole number</u> that multiplies by 5 to give 12.
When the base is <u>5 cm</u>, the height must be 12 ÷ 5 = <u>2.4 cm</u>.

Base	1 cm	2 cm	3 cm	4 cm	5 cm
Height	12 cm	6 cm	4 cm	3 cm	2.4 cm

? For each pair of values in Jack's table, draw two different parallelograms that Jack could have drawn.

EXAMPLE: A crocodile enclosure at a zoo is a parallelogram with base <u>15 m</u> and height <u>10 m</u>. The staff want to keep the area the same, but reduce the height to <u>2 m</u>. How long should the base be?

STEP 1: Calculate the <u>area</u> of the enclosure: 15 × 10 = 150 m²

STEP 2: Find the <u>base</u> of the <u>new</u> enclosure   150 = base × 2
— remember, the area stays the same.   So base = 150 ÷ 2 = <u>75 m</u>

You can also answer this question by looking at how the <u>height</u> has changed then do the <u>opposite</u> to the <u>base</u>:

The height is 10 ÷ 2 = <u>5</u> times <u>smaller</u>
so the base should be <u>5</u> times <u>bigger</u>.   15 × 5 = <u>75 m</u>

? What would the base be if the height was changed to 20 m? Can you solve this question in two different ways?

"I can calculate the area of a parallelogram."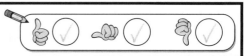

Perimeters and Areas

Different Shapes Can Have the Same Area...

... but they might have <u>different perimeters</u>.

EXAMPLE: A farmer needs a rectangular sheep pen with an area of <u>64 m²</u>. Each side should be a whole number of metres. What are the <u>smallest</u> and <u>largest</u> possible perimeters?

 Write down factor pairs of <u>64</u>. These <u>multiply</u> together to give the <u>area</u> of the sheep pen.

$$1\text{ m} \times 64\text{ m} \qquad 4\text{ m} \times 16\text{ m}$$
$$2\text{ m} \times 32\text{ m} \qquad 8\text{ m} \times 8\text{ m}$$

 Work out the <u>perimeter</u> of each of these rectangles.

1 m × 64 m: 1 + 64 + 1 + 64 = 130 m
2 m × 32 m: 2 + 32 + 2 + 32 = 68 m
4 m × 16 m: 4 + 16 + 4 + 16 = 40 m
8 m × 8 m: 8 + 8 + 8 + 8 = 32 m

You could draw a sketch of each rectangle to help work out the perimeter.

4 m
16 m

So the smallest perimeter is <u>32 m</u> and the largest perimeter is <u>130 m</u>.

Look at How Perimeter and Area are Linked

<u>Doubling</u> the <u>area</u> of a shape <u>doesn't</u> always mean that its <u>perimeter</u> doubles.

EXAMPLE:

Here is a 4 cm × 3 cm rectangle. Sketch a rectangle with <u>double</u> the <u>perimeter</u> and <u>double</u> the <u>area</u>.

3 cm
4 cm

1. Area of this rectangle = 4 × 3 = <u>12 cm²</u>
   Perimeter = 4 + 3 + 4 + 3 = <u>14 cm</u>

2. You want to find a rectangle with area 12 × 2 = <u>24 cm²</u> and perimeter 14 × 2 = <u>28 cm</u>.

   Are there any rectangles with an area of 24 cm² that don't have whole number side lengths? Are any of their perimeters 28 cm?

3. Whole number side lengths which give a <u>24 cm²</u> area are:
   1 cm × 24 cm, 2 cm × 12 cm,
   3 cm × 8 cm and 4 cm × 6 cm.

4. Work out the <u>perimeters</u> of each of these rectangles:
   1 cm × 24 cm: 1 + 24 + 1 + 24 = 50 cm ✗
   2 cm × 12 cm: 2 + 12 + 2 + 12 = <u>28 cm</u> ✓
   3 cm × 8 cm: 3 + 8 + 3 + 8 = 22 cm ✗
   4 cm × 6 cm: 4 + 6 + 4 + 6 = 20 cm ✗

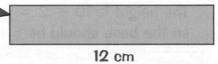

2 cm
12 cm

"I know that shapes with the same area can have different perimeters and vice versa."

Volumes of Cubes and Cuboids

You Can Fit Cubes into Bigger Cubes and Cuboids

The volume of a cube or cuboid is: length × width × height

EXAMPLE:

Ana's dice box is a 6 cm × 6 cm × 6 cm cube.
Her dice are 2 cm × 2 cm × 2 cm cubes.
How many dice can fit inside her dice box?

> Since 2 is a factor of 6, the dice will fit exactly along the length, width and height.

1. Find the volume of the dice box.   6 × 6 × 6 = 216 cm³
2. Find the volume of each dice.   2 × 2 × 2 = 8 cm³
3. Now divide: 216 ÷ 8 = 27 dice will fit in the box.

? Can you sketch out how they will be arranged?
Can you sketch out how they will be arranged?
What about if the dice were 1.5 cm cubes?

Some shapes don't fit neatly into larger containers so
you can't simply divide one volume by the other.
You have to think about how they'll fit in the container.

EXAMPLE: A plastic container is 7 cm × 5 cm × 3 cm.
A cube of cheese measures 2 cm × 2 cm × 2 cm.
How many cubes of cheese fit inside the plastic container?

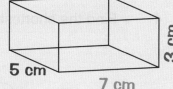

5 cm
7 cm
3 cm

1 Find the number of cheese cubes that will fit along the length:
7 ÷ 2 = 3.5, so 3 whole cheese cubes will fit.

2 Find the number of cubes that will fit along the width:
5 ÷ 2 = 2.5, so 2 whole cheese cubes will fit.

3 Find the number of cubes that will fit along the height:
3 ÷ 2 = 1.5, so 1 whole cheese cube will fit.

4 Multiply 3 × 2 × 1 = 6. ⟹ So 6 cheese cubes will fit inside the container.

? How many cheese cuboids measuring 1 cm × 2 cm × 2 cm would
fit inside the plastic container? It might help to do some sketches.

"I can calculate the volumes of cubes and cuboids."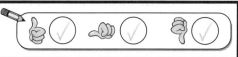

48

Practice Questions

1   There are 1000 milligrams in a gram. A shop is selling gold dust for £1 a bag. Each bag contains 100 milligrams of gold dust.

How much would it cost to buy 1.5 kg of gold dust from the shop?

2   Water is being poured into a 2 litre leaking bucket. Each second, 50 ml of water is being put into the bucket and 10 ml leaks out.

a)   How long will it take to fill the bucket to the top?

b)   How much longer would it take to fill if 30 ml leaked out every second?

3   Louise has made 2016 hours of phone calls since she first got her phone.

a)   How many minutes has she spent talking on her phone?

b)   How many weeks has she spent talking on her phone?

4   Find the shortest route between A and B on the map below.

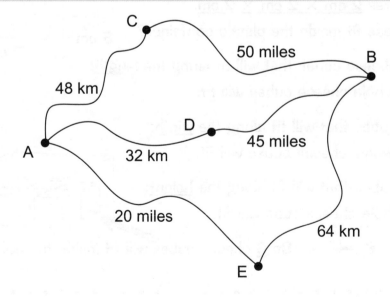

5   Draw three different triangles on a cm squared grid that all have an area of 8 cm².

Practice Questions

6 These two parallelograms have the same area. What is the missing length?

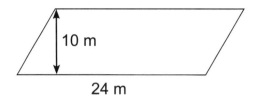

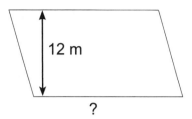

(Not drawn accurately)

7 Kara and Alyssa both own parallelogram-shaped paintings which have the same area. Kara's has a base of 6 m and height of 4 m.

The base of Alyssa's painting is one third of the base length of Kara's. What is the height of Alyssa's painting?

8 Andy is making a rectangular flag. He wants to add some beading to each edge. The area of the flag is 28 cm² and each edge is a whole number of cm long.

What is the smallest length of beading he will need?

9 Ann paints a wall 3 m high and 6 m wide. She then uses the same amount of paint to cover a wall that is 2 m high.

What is the difference in the perimeters of the two walls?

10 Aston's cuboid Turkish delight box measures 12 cm × 8 cm × 6 cm. It is filled with 2 cm cubes of Turkish delight.

How many cubes of Turkish delight does Aston have in his box?

11 Tea-rific Tea Rooms sells cube-shaped boxes of tea, with side length 7 cm. They are packed into crates for shipping, which measure 35 cm × 91 cm × 86 cm.

Find the maximum number of boxes of tea that can fit in each crate.

Drawing 2D Shapes

Use a Protractor to Help You Draw 2D Shapes

If you're given the <u>angles</u> and the <u>lengths</u> of the sides of a shape, use your protractor, a sharp pencil and a ruler to draw away...

> **EXAMPLE:** Draw triangle ABC accurately, where side AB = 5 cm, Angle A = 45° and angle B = 53°.

1 Draw <u>AB</u> first. This is <u>5 cm</u> long.

2 Use a protractor to draw angle <u>A</u>. This is <u>45°</u>. Draw a long line <u>away from</u> A.

3 Now use a protractor to draw angle <u>B</u>. This is <u>53°</u>. Draw a long line <u>away from</u> B.

4 The point where the lines cross is <u>C</u>.

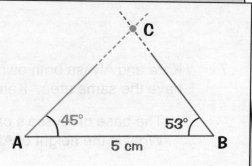

Some Triangles are Impossible to Draw

> **EXAMPLE:** Is it possible to draw this triangle accurately?

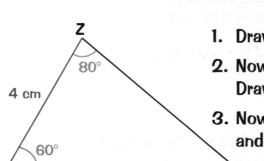

1. Draw the <u>line XY</u>.

2. Now measure <u>60°</u> to draw <u>angle X</u>. Draw a line <u>4 cm</u> long from X to make <u>line XZ</u>.

3. Now measure <u>80°</u> to draw <u>angle Z</u> and draw a straight line from <u>Z</u>.

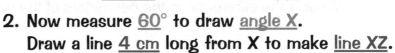

The sides of the triangle don't meet. So it is <u>impossible</u> to draw it accurately.

? How many different triangles can you draw that have a 5 cm side, a 6 cm side and a 50° angle?

"I can draw 2D shapes accurately."

Making 3D Shapes

3D Shapes Can Have More than One Net

There are often many <u>different</u> ways you can make a 3D shape.

EXAMPLE: Which of the nets below <u>does not</u> make a cube?

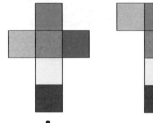 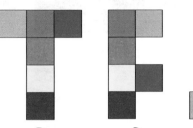

A   **B**   **C**   **D**

Each cube net should have <u>6 faces</u>. Visualise the net folding up and find the one that <u>doesn't work</u>.

<u>Net C</u> does not make a cube because the green and pink faces will fold on top of each other.

? How many other different nets can you sketch for a cube?

EXAMPLE: Draw three different nets to make this <u>pyramid</u>.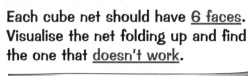

The shape has <u>one square face</u> and <u>four identical triangular faces</u>. Arrange these five shapes so they fold up to make a pyramid.

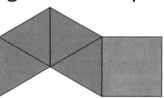 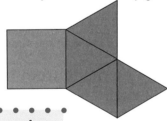 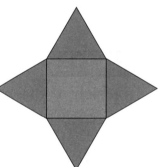

? Can you arrange the five faces so that they <u>don't</u> fold to make the pyramid?

EXAMPLE: Which of the following <u>is</u> the net for a <u>cylinder</u>?

A cylinder has <u>two circular faces</u> and one <u>rectangular face</u>.

A. 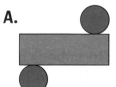   **B.** 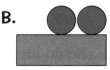   **C.**

The circles need to be on <u>opposite sides</u> of the rectangle and the sides they are touching need to be <u>long enough</u> to <u>wrap around</u> the circle.

<u>Net A</u> is the only net that will fold up into a cylinder.

"I can recognise, describe and build 3D shapes. I can make nets."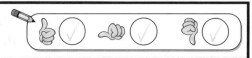

Making 3D Shapes

Visualise the Faces and Edges that Touch Each Other

Think about which <u>faces</u> are next to each other in a <u>3D shape</u> and which <u>edges</u> of a net will fold up to touch each other.

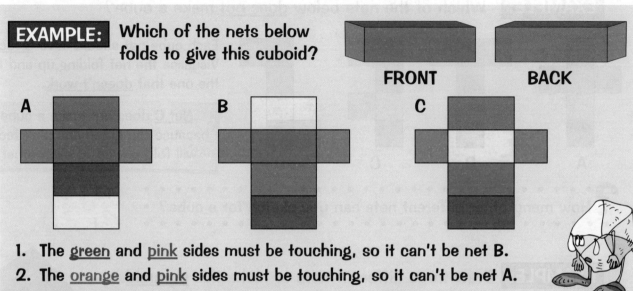

EXAMPLE: Which of the nets below folds to give this cuboid?

FRONT   BACK

A   B   C

1. The <u>green</u> and <u>pink</u> sides must be touching, so it can't be net B.
2. The <u>orange</u> and <u>pink</u> sides must be touching, so it can't be net A.
3. When net C is folded, the <u>pink</u> side will touch both the <u>orange</u> and <u>green</u> sides.

<u>Net C</u> will give this cuboid.

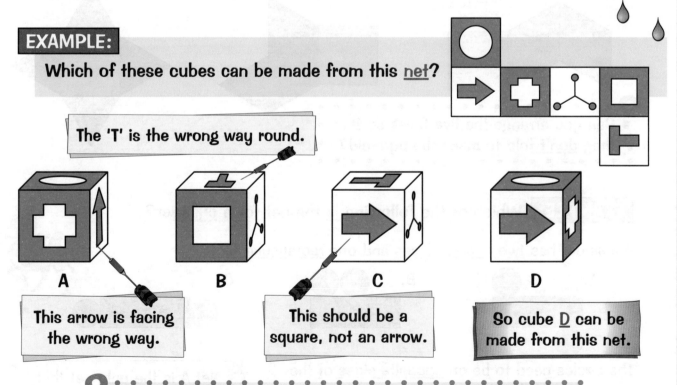

EXAMPLE:

Which of these cubes can be made from this <u>net</u>?

The 'T' is the wrong way round.

A   B   C   D

This arrow is facing the wrong way.

This should be a square, not an arrow.

So cube <u>D</u> can be made from this net.

? Draw possible nets that would fold to make cubes A, B and C.

"I can draw nets of 3D shapes. I can use nets to draw 3D shapes accurately."

SECTION SEVEN — GEOMETRY

Shape Properties

Some Shapes _Tessellate_ to Form _Patterns_

When shapes fit together with <u>no gaps</u>, they are said to <u>tessellate</u> — this happens when the <u>angles</u> at the point where the shapes meet <u>add up to 360°</u>.

EXAMPLE: Which <u>regular polygons</u> will make tessellating patterns?

The angles in a <u>regular polygon</u> are all the <u>same size</u> — if this angle goes exactly into 360°, then you'll get a <u>tessellating pattern</u>.

EQUILATERAL TRIANGLES

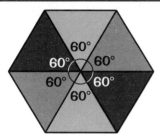

Interior angle = 60°
360° ÷ 60° = 6 triangles
around a point

SQUARES

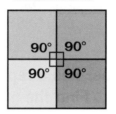

Interior angle = 90°
360° ÷ 90° = 4 squares
around a point

REGULAR HEXAGONS

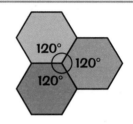

Interior angle = 120°
360° ÷ 120° = 3 hexagons
around a point

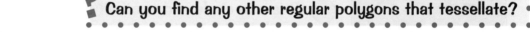
? Can you find any other regular polygons that tessellate?

Combine _Shapes_ to Make _Tessellating Patterns_

You can use <u>more than one</u> regular polygon to make tessellating patterns. For example, <u>squares</u> tessellate with <u>regular octagons</u>.

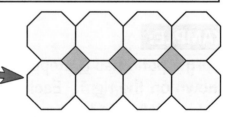

EXAMPLE:

Draw a tessellating pattern using <u>equilateral triangles</u> and <u>squares</u>.

At the point where the shapes meet, the angles add up to **360°**.
E.g. 60° + 60° + 60° + 90° + 90° = **360°**

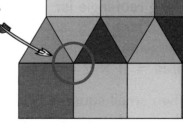

? Can you find any <u>irregular</u> polygons that could tessellate by themselves? Try the different quadrilaterals that you know.

"I know the properties of different shapes."

Circles

Use Circles to find Perimeters and Areas

Remember that <u>diameter = 2 × radius</u>.

EXAMPLE: Matthew's tray fits <u>4</u> identical glasses with no spaces between them, as shown below. Each glass has a <u>diameter</u> of <u>8 cm</u>. What is the <u>perimeter</u> of Matthew's tray?

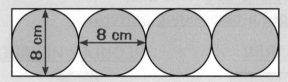

Length of tray: 4 × 8 cm = 32 cm

Width of tray: 1 × 8 cm = 8 cm

Perimeter: 32 + 8 + 32 + 8 = <u>80 cm</u>

EXAMPLE: Michal's wallpaper has a repeating pattern of circles, each with a <u>radius</u> of <u>10 cm</u>. Find the <u>area</u> of the sample of wallpaper shown.

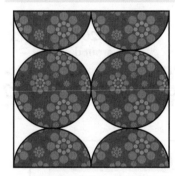

1. The sample is two circles wide.
   Each circle has a radius of 10 cm, so has a diameter of 2 × 10 = 20 cm. So the width is 20 + 20 = 40 cm.

2. It is one circle and two half circles high.
   So the height is 10 + 20 + 10 = 40 cm.

3. Now work out the area of the sample of wallpaper.

   Area: 40 × 40 = <u>160 cm²</u>

EXAMPLE:

Mary's patio has <u>6</u> stepping stones on it, as shown on the right. Each stone has a <u>radius</u> of <u>1 m</u>. What is the <u>area</u> of her patio?

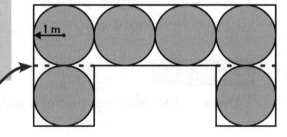

1. Split her patio up into a <u>long rectangle</u> along the top and <u>two small squares</u>.

2. The circles have diameters of 1 × 2 = 2 m.

3. The long rectangle is:
   4 circles long = 2 × 4 = 8 m
   1 circle wide = 2 m
   So area = 8 × 2 = 16 m²

How else could you split up Mary's patio to work out its area?

4. The two small squares have side lengths of 2 m.
   So they each have an area of 2 × 2 = 4 m².

Total area of patio
= 16 + 4 + 4 = <u>24 m²</u>

"I can name the parts of a circle and I know that the diameter of a circle is twice the length of its radius."

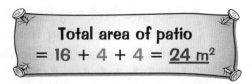

Angles in Shapes

Look for Certain Angles to Spot Impossible Shapes

Angles in a <u>triangle</u> add up to <u>180°</u> and angles in a <u>quadrilateral</u> add up to <u>360°</u>.

EXAMPLE: Ben has drawn and labelled some quadrilaterals below. Which of his shapes are impossible?

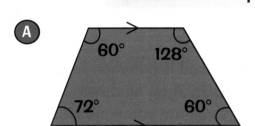

A

60°   128°

72°   60°

72° + 60° + 128° + 60° = 320°
so this quadrilateral is impossible.

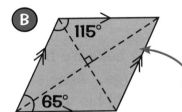

B

115°

65°

Opposite angles in a rhombus are equal. So the missing angles are 65° and 115°.

65° + 115° + 65° + 115° = 360°
so this quadrilateral is possible.

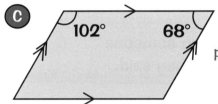

C

102°   68°

Opposite angles in a parallelogram are equal. So the missing angles are 68° and 102°.

102° + 68° + 102° + 68° = 340°
so this quadrilateral is impossible.

Shapes <u>A</u> and <u>C</u> are impossible.

? How could you change the angles in shape C so that it is possible?

EXAMPLE: Work out whether this triangle is impossible.

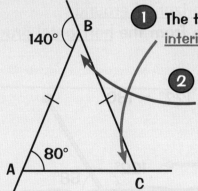

140°   B

80°

A   C

1 The triangle is <u>isosceles</u> so the <u>interior angle C</u> will also be <u>80°</u>.

2 Angles in a triangle add up to 180° so <u>interior angle B</u> = 180° − 80° − 80° = <u>20°</u>.

3 The angles at B are on a <u>straight line</u>, so they should add up to <u>180°</u>. But 140° + 20° = 160°.

So the triangle is <u>impossible</u>.

? Can you show that this triangle is impossible in another way using different angle rules?

"I can use my knowledge of shapes to find missing angles."

Angle Rules

Use Angle Rules To Find Missing Values

> Angles around a point add up to <u>360°</u>
> and angles on a straight line add up to <u>180°</u>.

EXAMPLES:

Alice baked a cake for her birthday. She shared it between herself, Amy and George. Alice said her slice was <u>90°</u>, Amy said hers was <u>40°</u> and George said his was <u>240°</u>. How do you know someone was lying?

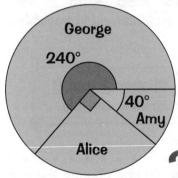

George 240°
40° Amy
Alice

Angles <u>around a point</u> should add up to <u>360°</u>.
$90° + 40° + 240° = \underline{370°}$

370° is bigger than 360° so someone must have eaten less than they said.

George actually ate half of what he said and Alice ate twice as much as she said. How much did Amy eat?

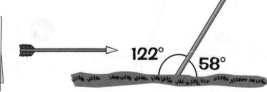

The wind has blown over a flag pole.
Taz says that it's at a <u>58°</u> angle from the <u>horizontal ground</u>.
Wilson says that it's actually at a <u>122°</u> angle from the <u>horizontal ground</u>.
Explain how they could <u>both</u> be correct.

Angles on a straight line add up to 180°. $58° + 122° = 180°$

So Taz and Wilson could be measuring <u>different sides</u> of the <u>same angle</u> with the horizontal ground.

122°   58°

What angle would Taz say that the flag pole needed to move to make it vertical again? Would Wilson agree with him?

"I can use rules to find missing angles."

Coordinates

Work Out Missing Coordinates of Shapes

You can use your knowledge of <u>shapes</u> to work out <u>missing coordinates</u>.

EXAMPLE: Joe wants to draw a right-angled triangle on a grid.
He draws one side between point A at (–1, 6) and point B at (3, –4).
Where could he draw the third corner, point C?

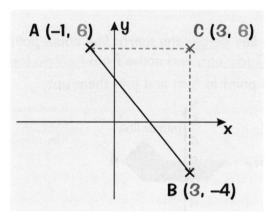

Point C could line up <u>horizontally</u> with **A**.
So they will have the same <u>y-coordinate</u>.

Point C could line up <u>vertically</u> with **B**.
So they will have the same <u>x-coordinate</u>.

So point C could be drawn at (3, 6).

? Where else could point C be drawn?

EXAMPLE: Harry has buried a surprise for Molly.
She can find the surprise by following his clues on a grid:

Draw a rectangle here for all to see,
And label the corners D, E, F and G.
Point D should be drawn at coordinates (4, 2),
Then move down to draw E, it's at (4, –2).
Move across to point F at (–2, –2),
Then find the last corner —
        you know what to do.
Finally, the surprise lies at the place,
Where the diagonals meet —
        now you've solved the case!

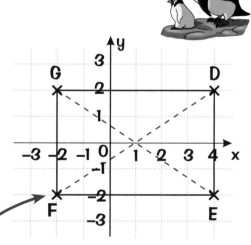

1. Draw the points <u>D</u>, <u>E</u>, <u>F</u> and <u>G</u> by following the clues. G will line up <u>vertically with F</u> and <u>horizontally with D</u> since the shape is a <u>rectangle</u>.

2. Draw the <u>diagonals</u> from <u>G to E</u> and from <u>D to F</u>.

3. The surprise will be where they meet. → The surprise is at (1, 0).

"I can use coordinates in four quadrants."

Reflection

Reflect Shapes and Patterns in a Mirror Line

When you reflect shapes in a mirror line, each <u>point</u> of the <u>reflection</u> should be exactly the <u>same distance</u> away from the mirror line as the points on the <u>original shape</u>.

EXAMPLE: Reflect the shape below in the <u>y-axis</u>.
What are the new <u>coordinates</u> of vertex D?

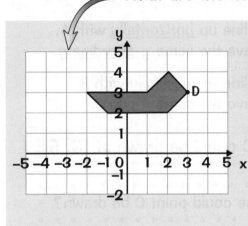

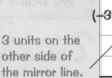

Because the shape lies <u>across</u> the mirror line some points will reflect from <u>left to right</u>, and some from <u>right to left</u>.

Plot each reflected point in turn and join them up:

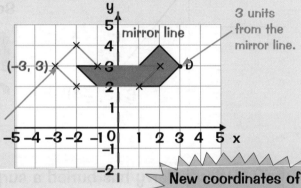

3 units from the mirror line.

3 units on the other side of the mirror line.

New coordinates of vertex D = <u>(–3, 3)</u>

? What do you notice about the coordinates of each corner before and after it has been reflected?

EXAMPLE: <u>Reflect</u> the design below in the <u>x-axis</u>.

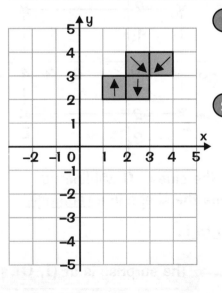

1. As usual, <u>reflect each vertex</u> of the shape in turn, and <u>join them up</u> to form the reflection.

2. You also need to think about how the <u>arrow design</u> would look when it's <u>reflected</u>.
E.g. if the arrow in the <u>original design</u> is pointing <u>towards</u> the mirror line, the arrow in the <u>reflected image</u> will also point <u>towards</u> the mirror line.

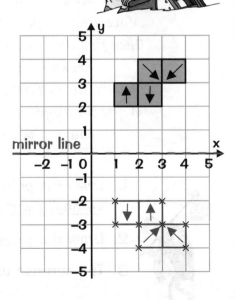

"I can reflect a shape in the axes of a grid and give the coordinates of the image."

Translation

You Can Translate Shapes to Make New Shapes

Remember:

> A **positive** number translates a shape **right** or **up**.
>
> A **negative** number translates a shape **left** or **down**.

EXAMPLE:

Mark decides to move his house. He attaches balloons to it, and flies it to the top of a hill, as shown. Describe the translation.

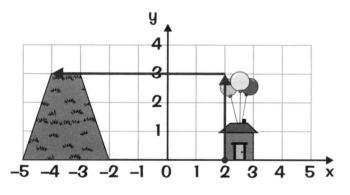

Pick a point on the house to look at — such as the bottom left corner.

The point moves **3 squares up**...

... and **6 squares left**.

So any point of the translation can be given by: **(x – 6, y + 3)**.

EXAMPLE: Translate triangles A and B on the grid below to create a rectangle with one of its corners at point (–1, 1).

Draw in the rectangle first, then work out how to translate A and B to make it.

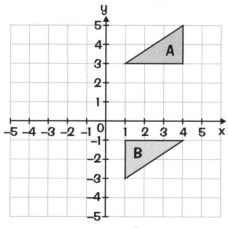

Translate triangle A
2 units down and
5 units left.

Translate triangle B
5 units left and
4 units up.

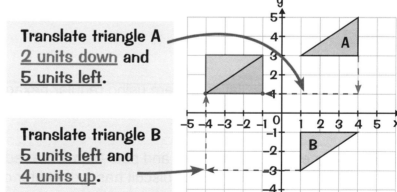

? How many different answers can you find for this example?
What if you were making a parallelogram with a corner at (1, 2)?

"I can translate shapes using coordinates."

Practice Questions

1 Decide if each of these triangles can be drawn accurately.

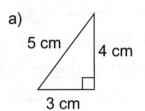
a)
5 cm
4 cm
3 cm

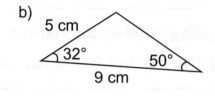
b)
5 cm
32°
50°
9 cm

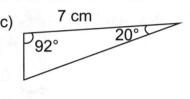
c)
7 cm
92°
20°

2 Which of the following nets does <u>not</u> make a cuboid?

A 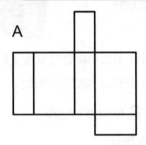   B 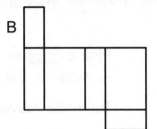   C 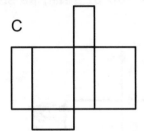   D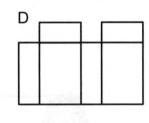

3 This 3D shape is made up of 3 identical cubes.
Complete the net with the correct faces of the cubes.

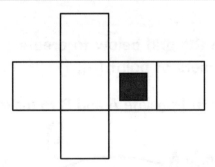

4 Draw a tessellating pattern using regular hexagons and equilateral triangles.

5 Eimear has ten biscuits and puts them on a rectangular plate,
as shown below. Each biscuit has a diameter of 5 cm.

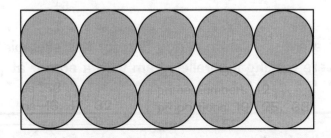

What is the area of her plate?

Practice Questions

6   The exterior angles of any polygon add up to 360°.
Use this fact to decide whether the shape sketched below is a regular polygon.

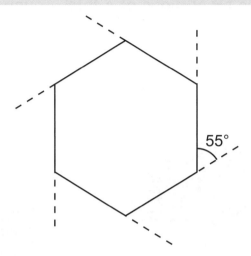

7   Look at the grid to the right.

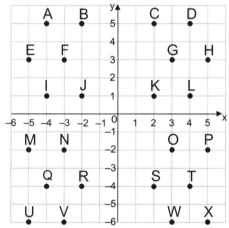

a)   Write the word spelt by the letters with the
coordinates: (4, 5) (−2, −4) (−4, 5) (3, −6).

b)   E is reflected in the y-axis.
Which point is it on the grid?

c)   T is translated 5 units up and 2 units left.
Which point does it land on?

d)   A rectangle has vertices at C, I and K.
Give the letter of the other vertex, and the
coordinates of the point where the diagonals cross.

8   Look at the shape drawn on this grid.

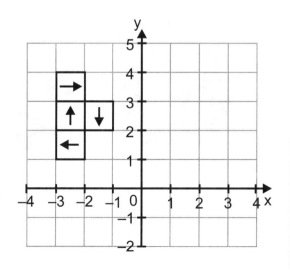

a)   Reflect the shape in the y-axis.

b)   Translate one square of the original
shape to make the shape below.
Describe the translation.

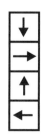

Pie Charts

You Can Compare Pie Charts When the Totals are Equal

Pie charts show things as proportions of a total — you can easily compare them when the totals of the pie charts are the same.

EXAMPLE: Emily and John both spent 8 hours at a theme park. The pie charts below show how they spent their time.

Emily spent half her time on the rides — that's 4 hours.

Emily spent less time eating than John.

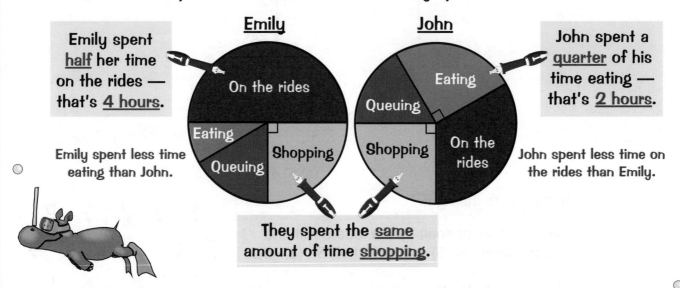

John spent a quarter of his time eating — that's 2 hours.

John spent less time on the rides than Emily.

They spent the same amount of time shopping.

But Be Careful When the Totals are Different

Watch out when the totals aren't the same. Even if the proportions of the pie charts are the same, the amounts they represent are not.

EXAMPLE: All 48 pupils in Year 5 and all 36 pupils in Year 6 were asked if they had ever been snorkelling. Which year had more snorkelers?

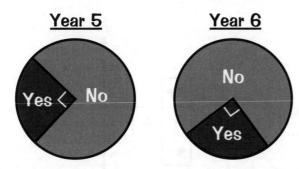

One quarter of Year 5 had been snorkelling: 48 ÷ 4 = 12 snorkelers.

One quarter of Year 6 had been snorkelling: 36 ÷ 4 = 9 snorkelers.

So Year 5 has more snorkelers.

? Why is it difficult to compare pie charts when you don't know their totals?

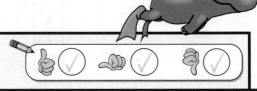

"I understand what pie charts show."

Pie Charts

Draw a Pie Chart By Working Out the Angles

You can use fractions and percentages to help draw pie charts
— they tell you the proportions of the pie.

EXAMPLE:

Oscar the rabbit spends 8 hours of the day sleeping, $\frac{1}{5}$ of the day cleaning
his cage, 10% of the day eating and the rest of the day sunbathing.
Draw a pie chart to show Oscar's day.

① Find the angle that represents each activity.

Sleeping: $\frac{8}{24} = \frac{1}{3}$ *There are 24 hours in a day, so he spends a third of the day sleeping.*

$\frac{1}{3}$ of 360 = 360° ÷ 3 = <u>120</u>°

Cleaning: $\frac{1}{5}$ of 360 = 360° ÷ 5 = <u>72</u>°

Eating: 10% of 360 = 360° ÷ 10 = <u>36</u>°

② Draw and label the pie chart.

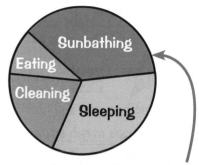

You don't need to work out
the last sector — it'll just
be the piece that's left.

? How could you work out how much
time Oscar spent sunbathing?

Finding the Total of a Pie Chart

Once you know the angle of a sector and the amount it represents,
you can work out the total number that the pie chart shows.

EXAMPLE:

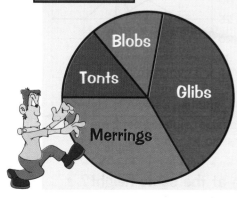

Tom draws a pie chart to show each type of monster
he defeats in his new computer game. He defeats
<u>70</u> Glibs, and his sector for Glibs measures <u>140</u>°.
How many monsters did he defeat in total?

1) 140° = 70 monsters. 140° ÷ 70 = <u>2</u>° per monster.

2) There are 360° in a pie chart,
so 360° ÷ 2° = 180 monsters.

> Tom defeats
> <u>180</u> monsters
> in total.

"I can draw and interpret pie charts."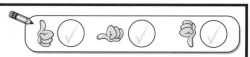

Line Graphs

Draw Two Line Graphs to Compare Data

You can draw <u>two lines</u> on the <u>same graph</u> when comparing <u>similar</u> things or situations.

EXAMPLE: Jane and Michael are each flying a kite. They record how high their kites are flying every minute, as shown in the table below.

	Minute 1	Minute 2	Minute 3	Minute 4	Minute 5
Jane	21 m	20 m	32 m	25 m	25 m
Michael	25 m	30 m	25 m	0 m	0 m

 1 Create a <u>line graph</u> for their data. Put both lines on the same graph.

The <u>scale</u> should be big enough for <u>both</u> sets of data.

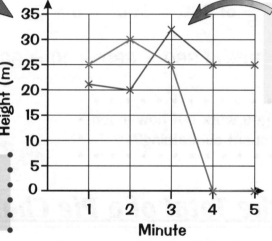

Choose a different <u>colour</u> for each line and write a key.

? What does it mean when the graph touches the horizontal axis?

2 Between which times were both Jane and Michael's kites at the same height?

Look at the graph to find where the lines <u>cross</u>.

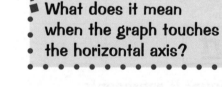

They are at the same height between <u>2 and 3 minutes</u>.

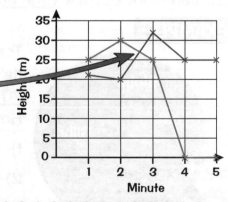

? Is this the only time the kites could have been at the same height?

"I can interpret and construct line graphs."

The Mean

Use the Mean to Work Out the Total

To work out the <u>mean</u> of some numbers — <u>add up</u> the numbers
and <u>divide</u> the total by <u>how many</u> numbers there are.
If you know the <u>mean</u>, you can work backwards to find the <u>total</u>.

EXAMPLES:

① A zoo has <u>30</u> green flamingos. Their <u>mean</u> height is <u>1.2 m</u>.
What is the <u>total height</u> of all the green flamingos?

The <u>mean</u> is the total height ÷ number of flamingos,
so the <u>total height</u> is the mean × number of flamingos:

Total height = 1.2 × 30 = <u>36 m</u>

② The zoo bought <u>10</u> blue flamingos. Their mean height was <u>1.6 m</u>.
What is the <u>mean height</u> of all <u>40</u> flamingos?

<u>Total</u> height of <u>blue</u> flamingos = 1.6 × 10 = <u>16 m</u>

<u>Total</u> height of <u>all 40</u> flamingos = 36 m + 16 m = 52 m

So the <u>mean height</u> of <u>all</u> the flamingos is 52 m ÷ 40 = <u>1.3 m</u>

Work Out Missing Values Using the Mean

EXAMPLE:
Declan has grown four weeds. Their <u>mean</u> height is <u>8 cm</u>.
The table below shows the heights of <u>three</u> of the weeds.
What is the height of the <u>fourth</u> weed?

<u>STEP 1</u> The <u>total height</u> of all four weeds
will be 8 cm × 4 = <u>32 cm</u>.

<u>STEP 2</u> The total height of weeds 1, 2 and 3
is 10 + 12 + 4 = <u>26 cm</u>.

<u>STEP 3</u> The height of weed 4 is the difference
between the totals: 32 − 26 = <u>6 cm</u>.

Weed	Height (cm)
Weed 1	10
Weed 2	12
Weed 3	4
Weed 4	?

Declan grows another two weeds. The mean height of all 6 weeds is 10 cm.
How tall are weeds 5 and 6? Write down as many possible answers as you can.

"I know what the mean is.
I can calculate and use the mean."

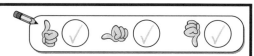

Practice Questions

1   Ed and Chris got £20 each for their birthday. Kim got £30 for her birthday.
The pie charts below show how they all spent their money.

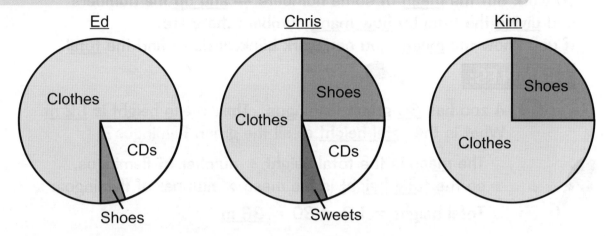

a)   Why is it easy to compare the pie charts for Ed and Chris?

b)   Kim says she spent the same amount of money as Ed on clothes.
Is she correct?

2   A group of people were asked to choose either chocolate cake or lemon cake.
The results were put in a pie chart. 80 people chose chocolate cake.

The sector for chocolate cake measured 240°.
How many people chose lemon cake?

3   Matt asks a group of people what colour their car is.
He records their answers in a table, ready to put in a pie chart.

Car colour	Number of people	Angle
Red	16	64°
Blue	25	
White		152°
Other	11	

a)   How many people did Matt ask in total?

b)   Complete the table by working out the missing values.

c)   Use your table to draw a pie chart of his data.

SECTION EIGHT — STATISTICS

4   36 people went to a fancy dress party. $\frac{1}{6}$ of them dressed up as pirates, 25% dressed as ninjas, 12 of them dressed as zombies and the rest didn't dress up.

Draw a pie chart to show the proportions of people in different costumes.

5   Kay wants to compare how much her llama and alpaca increase in weight over 6 weeks. The table below shows their weights at the end of each week.

	Week 1	Week 2	Week 3	Week 4	Week 5	Week 6
Weight of llama (kg)	20	26	35	32	32	38
Weight of alpaca (kg)	8	16	28	36	40	40

a)   Draw a line graph to show Kay's data. Draw both lines on the same graph.

b)   What happened to the alpaca's weight during the sixth week?

c)   During which week did the llama and the alpaca weigh the same?

6   20 runners take part in an egg-and-spoon race.
Their mean finishing time is 23.4 seconds.

What is the total race time for all of the runners?

7   A lift can hold a maximum of 800 kg. There are 6 men and 5 women in the lift. The mean weight for men is 84 kg and the mean weight for women is 55 kg.

Is the total weight of the people in the lift above the maximum weight?

8   The mean of the following group of numbers is 9. Find the missing value.

     8,   3,   19,   13,   ?

Answers

Page 6 — Section One

1) a) Each small step is 1 000 000 ÷ 5 = 200 000.
So half a small step is worth
200 000 ÷ 2 = 100 000.
The arrow is pointing to one and a half steps
above 7 000 000:
7 000 000 + 200 000 + 100 000 = **7 300 000**

b) A quarter of a small step is worth
200 000 ÷ 4 = 50 000.
The arrow is pointing to three and a quarter
steps above 7 000 000:
7 000 000 + (3 × 200 000) + 50 000
= 7 000 000 + 600 000 + 50 000
= **7 650 000**

2) a)

Box	Number of Crayons	Highest Possible Number of Crayons	Lowest Possible Number of Crayons
A	500 (to the nearest 100)	**549**	**450**
B	470 (to the nearest 10)	**474**	**465**
C	476 exactly	**476**	**476**
D	1000 (to the nearest 1000)	**1499**	**500**

b) No — there are no boxes where the lowest
possible amount is higher than the highest
possible amount in all the other boxes.

3) a) To get from 8 to 4 you need to subtract 4,
which is the same as adding **−4**.

b) To get from 32 to 16 you need to subtract 16,
which is the same as adding **−16**.

c) Reordering gives −6 + 21 + ☐ = 4 which
simplifies to 15 + ☐ = 4.
To get from 15 to 4 you subtract 11,
which is the same as adding **−11**.

4) −7 + 15 = **8 °C** and −7 − 15 = **−22 °C**

5) Pairs of odd digits that add up to 10 are:
1 and 9, 3 and 7, 5 and 5
Only 3 and 7 have a difference of 4, so the
number Georgio is thinking of could be **37** or **73**.

Pages 14-15 — Section Two

1)
```
    2  8 [4] 5  3
  ×         3 [2]
   [5] 6  9  0  6
  8  5  3 [5] 9  0
  ─────────────────
 [9] 1  0  4  9 [6]
```

2) ☐☐☐☐ × ☐ = 54072 is the
same as 54072 ÷ ☐ = ☐☐☐☐.
Try each of the digits 5-9 in turn as the divisor to
find which gives an answer containing the other
digits: 54072 ÷ 8 = 6759.

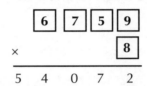
```
  [6][7][5][9]
  ×         [8]
  ─────────────
   5  4  0  7  2
```

3) a)
```
        4 8 remainder 23
   50 )2 4 2⁴²3
```
Teo will walk past **48 lamp posts** on his walk.

b) The distance between the last lamp post and
the beach is **23 m**.

4) Louis puts 72 − 7 = 65 books into boxes.
So the number of boxes he uses will be
a factor of 65: 1, 5, 13 or 65.
Removing all the factors less than 7 leaves
13 and 65. Since each box has more than
1 book in it, Louis uses **13** boxes.

5) 456 ÷ 8 = (400 + 56) ÷ 8 = 50 + 7 = **57 cm**

6) 343 = 300 + 40 + 3
So 6244 + 300 + 40 + 3 = 6587
452 = 400 + 50 + 2
So 6587 − 400 − 50 − 2 = **6135 ml**

7) 100 × 20 = 2000
100 × 16 = 1600
98 × 20 = 1960
So **100 × 16** is the closest estimate.

8) E.g. £17.95 ≈ £20 and 27 ≈ 30 months
£20 × 30 = £600

Both values were rounded up so the actual value
will be less than £600. So Monika is **wrong**.

9) a) 24 − 2 + 3 × 4 = 24 − 2 + 12 = 22 + 12 = **34**

b) 39 + 6 ÷ 2 − 4 = 39 + 3 − 4 = 42 − 4 = **38**

c) 63 + 3 − 8 × (2 + 4) = 63 + 3 − 8 × 6
= 63 + 3 − 48 = 66 − 48 = **18**

10) a) 3 + 7 × (5 − 1) = 31

b) 16 ÷ (4 − 2) + 23 = 31

c) 24 − (1 + 2) × 4 = 12

d) 30 ÷ (10 ÷ 5 + 4) = 5

11) The number of blocks divides by 20 and 8,
so find a common multiple of 20 and 8.
Multiples of 20 that are less than 100:
20, 40, 60, 80

Answers

Multiples of 8 that are less than 100:
8, 16, 24, 32, 40, 48, 56, 64, 72, 80, 88, 96
So he could have **40** or **80** building blocks.

12) Some years are leap years which have a 29th of February (29/2). This is a prime date so Jane is **correct**.

13) 120 ÷ 3 = 40 m of blue wool
40 ÷ 2 = 20 m left after knitting the scarf
20 − 15 = **5 m** left when she's finished knitting

14) 374 × £12 = £4488 in advance tickets
126 ÷ 2 = 63
63 × £15 = £945 in standard tickets
63 × £20 = £1260 in VIP tickets
So £4488 + £945 + £1260 = **£6693**

Pages 26-27 — Section Three

1) Find equivalent fractions to $\frac{2}{13}$ that have denominators less than 50.

$$\frac{2}{13} = \frac{4}{26} = \frac{6}{39}$$

Linda could've taken either **2, 4** or **6 chocolates**.

2) Cross multiply to check for equivalence:

$\frac{2}{7}$ and $\frac{12}{49}$: 2 × 49 = 98 and 7 × 12 = 84
so they are not equivalent.

$\frac{3}{9}$ and $\frac{11}{33}$: 3 × 33 = 99 and 9 × 11 = 99
so they **are equivalent**.

$\frac{7}{11}$ and $\frac{77}{110}$: 7 × 110 = 770 and 11 × 77 = 847
so they are not equivalent.

$\frac{15}{24}$ and $\frac{35}{56}$: 15 × 56 = 840 and 24 × 35 = 840
so they **are equivalent**.

3) Divide the number line into twelfths:

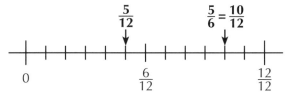

4) Add up the mixed numbers using the method you find easiest, for example:

$3\frac{2}{3} + 2\frac{2}{5} + 1\frac{5}{6} = 3 + 2 + 1 + \frac{2}{3} + \frac{2}{5} + \frac{5}{6}$

$= 6 + \frac{20}{30} + \frac{12}{30} + \frac{25}{30}$

$= 6 + \frac{57}{30} = 6 + 1\frac{27}{30} = 7\frac{27}{30} = 7\frac{9}{10}$

Michelle's project is $7\frac{9}{10}$ **pages**
so it is **not** too long.

5) After spending $\frac{1}{4}$ of his money, Stan is left with $\frac{3}{4}$.

So you need to find $\frac{7}{9}$ of $\frac{3}{4}$: $\frac{3}{4} \times \frac{7}{9} = \frac{21}{36} = \frac{7}{12}$.

6) Option 1: $\frac{3}{5} \div 8 = \frac{3}{40} = \frac{6}{80}$ of the sand per wall

Option 2: $\frac{7}{8} \div 10 = \frac{7}{80}$ of the sand per wall

So there will be more sand per wall if she takes $\frac{7}{8}$ **and builds 10 identical walls**.

7)
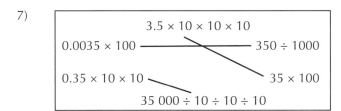

8) a) Estimate: 12 ÷ 12 = 1 kg — this is close to 0.96 kg so the statement **could be true**.

b) Estimate: 60 × 3 m = 180 m — this is very different from 1624.23 m so the statement is **definitely false**.

9) **No.** His time could have been 9.624 which is slower than the record.

10) Continue the pattern — the decimal form of each fraction are repeating multiples of 9:
0.0̲90909..., 0.1̲81818..., 0.2̲72727... so:

$\frac{4}{11} = \mathbf{0.\underline{36}3636...}$, $\frac{5}{11} = \mathbf{0.\underline{45}4545...}$

and $\frac{6}{11} = \mathbf{0.\underline{54}5454...}$

11) Time is usually given in fractions so:
2.25 hours = $2\frac{1}{4}$ hours.

Money is usually given as a decimal so:
$£5\frac{3}{20} = £5\frac{15}{100} = £5.15$

My best friend said that in $2\frac{1}{4}$ hours the local clothing shop is selling all of its sweaters for **£5.15** each.

Pages 34-35 — Section Four

1) One pair of socks costs £12.60 ÷ 6 = £2.10
£21 is equal to 10 × £2.10
So he can buy **10 pairs of socks** with £21.

2) a) 800 g ÷ 4 = 200 g of marrow per portion
2400 g ÷ 200 g = 12
So Ruth can make **12 portions** of stew.

b) She makes 12 portions, but the recipe is for 4 portions. 12 ÷ 4 = 3, so multiply all the other ingredients by 3.

500 g × 3 = **1500 g tomatoes**
1.2 litres × 3 = **3.6 litres vegetable stock**
250 g × 3 = **750 g mushrooms**

Answers

3) The scale is 50 cm = 35 m,
so 1 cm = 35 ÷ 50 = 0.7 m.
Multiply the length by 0.7: 57 × 0.7 = 39.9
so the length of the real plane is **39.9 m**

4) a) Height of shape A = 4 units
Height of shape B = 12 units
Scale factor = 12 ÷ 4 = **3**

b) E.g.

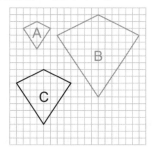

5) Green coat:
1% of £300 = £300 ÷ 100 = £3
57% of £300 = £3 × 57 = £171
The green coat costs £171 so
he is saving £300 − £171 = £129.

Orange coat:
50% of £160 = £160 ÷ 2 = £80
25% of £160 = £160 ÷ 4 = £40
75% of £160 = £80 + £40 = £120
The orange coat costs £120 so
he is saving £160 − £120 = £40.

So either: "Tom should buy the green coat
because it's a bigger saving" or "Tom should buy
the orange coat because it is still cheaper."

6) There are 32 + 23 + 9 = 64 people in Year 5 and
29 + 4 + 17 = 50 people in Year 6.

% of Year 5 who said yes = $\frac{32}{64}$ = $\frac{1}{2}$ = 50%

% of Year 6 who said yes = $\frac{29}{50}$ = $\frac{58}{100}$ = 58%

A higher percentage of Year 6 pupils are going
to the disco so Taylor is wrong.

7) For every 2 stickers that Ben gets, Shaun gets
3 stickers and Adam gets 2 ÷ 2 = 1 sticker.

So there are 2 + 3 + 1 = 6 shares in total.

90 ÷ 6 = 15 stickers for one share.
Adam gets 1 share, so gets 1 × 15 = 15 stickers.
Shaun gets 3 shares, so gets 3 × 15 = 45 stickers.
So Shaun gets 45 − 15 = **30 more stickers**
than Adam.

8) He uses 2 × 2 = 4 parts orange juice,
so 3 + 2 + 4 = 9 parts in total.

270 ml ÷ 9 = 30 ml per part.
He uses 3 parts pineapple juice
so 30 ml × 3 = **90 ml**.

Pages 40-41 — Section Five

1) a) add 2.5   b) subtract $\frac{1}{4}$

2) a) The rule is 'add $\frac{3}{4}$', so the sequence
continues: 2, $2\frac{3}{4}$, $3\frac{1}{2}$, $4\frac{1}{4}$, 5, $5\frac{3}{4}$, $6\frac{1}{2}$, $7\frac{1}{4}$

b) The rule is 'subtract 3.5', so the sequence
continues: 11, 7.5, 4, 0.5, −3, −6.5,
−10, −13.5... so the 8th term is **−13.5**

3) 5, 11, 23, 47, 95

4) a) 6 + 7 = **13**

b) 3 × 8 − 7 = 24 − 7 = **17**

c) 2 × 6 − 7 + 4 × 8 = 12 − 7 + 32 = **37**

5) a) **p** + **r** = 11 or **r** + **p** = 11

b) 4**r** − **s** = 17

c) **p** × **s** − **r** = 13 or **s** × **p** − **r** = 13

6) G + G + G + G = 16, so G = 4
G + G + H + H = 14, so H = 3
G + H + H + K = 12, so K = 2

G	H	H	K	12
G	K	K	K	**10**
G	G	H	H	14
G	K	K	H	**11**
16	**11**	**10**	**10**	

7) She bought a total of 18 items so b + g = 18.
She bought 4 more books than games so b − g = 4.
Find pairs of numbers that make b + g = 18
correct then check to see if b − g = 4:
11 + 7 = 18 and 11 − 7 = 4
So she bought **11 books** and **7 games**.

8) A = 2B, A + B = 60p, B + C = 50p
If A is twice the cost of B then A + B must be
three times the cost of B. So B = 60p ÷ 3 = **20p**.
This means that A = 2 × 20p = **40p** and
C = 50p − 20p = **30p**.

9) Number of badges = 50 + 2 × number of times
she cuts the grass in a year

10) a) Pattern 1: 4 × 1 − ☐ = 1 circle, so 4 − ☐ = 1
Pattern 2: 4 × 2 − ☐ = 5 circles, so 8 − ☐ = 5
Pattern 3: 4 × 3 − ☐ = 9 circles, so 12 − ☐ = 9
The missing number in each of these is 3, so:
Number of circles = 4 × pattern number − 3

b) Number of circles = 4 × 30 − 3 = **117**

Answers

Pages 48-49 — Section Six

1) 1.5 kg of gold dust is the same as
$1.5 \times 1000 = 1500$ g
$1500 \times 1000 = 1\ 500\ 000$ mg

The number of bags needed is
$1\ 500\ 000$ mg $\div 100 = 15\ 000$ bags

Each bag costs £1 so it would cost **£15 000**
for 1.5 kg of gold dust.

2) a) 50 ml is being added and 10 ml is leaving the
bucket, so in total
$50 - 10 = 40$ ml is being added every second.
2 litres $= 2 \times 1000 = 2000$ ml
So it will take $2000 \div 40 =$ **50 seconds**
to fill the bucket.

b) Now 30 ml is leaking out so in total
$50 - 30 = 20$ ml is being added every second.
So it will take $2000 \div 20 = 100$ seconds to fill.
This is $100 - 50 =$ **50 seconds longer**.

3) a) There are 60 minutes in an hour, so
2016 hours $= 2016 \times 60 =$ **120 960 minutes**.

b) There are 24 hours in a day, so
2016 hours $= 2016 \div 24 = 84$ days
There are 7 days in a week, so
84 days $= 84 \div 7 =$ **12 weeks**.

4) A to B via C
48 km $+ (50 \div 5 \times 8)$ km $= 48 + 80 = 128$ km
A to B via D
32 km $+ (45 \div 5 \times 8)$ km $= 32 + 72 = 104$ km
A to B via E
$(20 \div 5 \times 8)$ km $+ 64$ km $= 32 + 64 = 96$ km
So route **A to B via E** is shortest.

5) Any three triangles with bases and heights that
multiply together to give 16, e.g.
Base = 1 cm and height = 16 cm
Base = 2 cm and height = 8 cm
Base = 4 cm and height = 4 cm

6) Area of first parallelogram: $10 \times 24 = 240$ m².
So base of second parallelogram:
$240 \div 12 =$ **20 m**

7) Area of Kara's painting: $6 \times 4 = 24$ m²
Base of Alyssa's painting: $6 \div 3 = 2$ m
So height of Alyssa's painting: $24 \div 2 =$ **12 m**

8) There are three possible rectangles:
1 cm × 28 cm, 2 cm × 14 cm and 4 cm × 7 cm.

1 cm × 28 cm: $1 + 28 + 1 + 28 = 58$ cm
2 cm × 14 cm: $2 + 14 + 2 + 14 = 32$ cm
4 cm × 7 cm: $4 + 7 + 4 + 7 = 22$ cm
So the smallest length of beading = **22 cm**

9) Perimeter of first wall: $3 + 6 + 3 + 6 = 18$ m
Area of first wall: $3 \times 6 = 18$ m²
This is also the area of the second wall,
so width of second wall: $18 \div 2 = 9$ m
Perimeter of second wall: $2 + 9 + 2 + 9 = 22$ m
So the difference in perimeters $= 22 - 18 =$ **4 m**

10) 2 goes into 12, 8 and 6,
so they will fit exactly.
Volume of cuboid box: $12 \times 8 \times 6 = 576$ cm²
Volume of a cube of Turkish delight:
$2 \times 2 \times 2 = 8$ cm²
$576 \div 8 =$ **72 cubes of Turkish delight**.

11) Number of boxes along length: $35 \div 7 = 5$
Number of boxes along width: $91 \div 7 = 13$
Number of boxes along height: $86 \div 7 = 12$ r 2
So $5 \times 13 \times 12 =$ **780 boxes of tea** will fit.

Pages 60-61 — Section Seven

1) Draw each triangle using a ruler and protractor.

a) **Yes**, triangle a) can be drawn accurately.

b) **No**, triangle b) cannot be drawn accurately.

c) **Yes**, triangle c) can be drawn accurately.

2) **Net D** does not make a cuboid.

3) There are several different nets you could draw,
e.g.

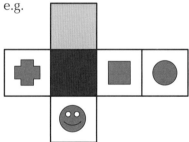

4) There are lots of patterns you could draw — here
are some examples:

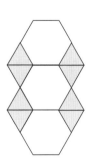 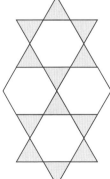

Answers

5) Length of plate = 5 × 5 cm = 25 cm
Width of plate = 2 × 5 cm = 10 cm
Area of plate = 25 cm × 10 cm = **250 cm²**

6) In a regular shape, all the exterior angles
are equal and add up to 360°.
If all the exterior angles of this hexagon were 55°
then the total would be 55° × 6 = 330° which is
less than 360°. So the hexagon is **irregular**.

7) a) DRAW

b) H (5, 3)

c) K (2, 1)

d) The other vertex is at **A (–4, 5)** and the
diagonals cross at **(–1, 3)**.

8) a)
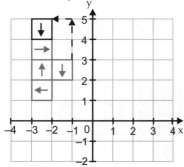

b) Translate the downward arrow square
two units up and one unit left.

Pages 66-67 — Section Eight

1) a) Because both pie charts have the same total
(£20), so the same sized sector represents the
same amount.

b) E.g. no because Kim spent $\frac{3}{4}$ of £30 = £22.50
and Ed spent $\frac{3}{4}$ of £20 = £15, so their totals
are not the same.

2) 240° = 80 people, so 240° ÷ 80 = 3° per person.
360° ÷ 3° = 120 people in total
So 120 – 80 = **40** people chose lemon cake.

3) a) 64° = 16, so 64° ÷ 16 = 4° per person
360° ÷ 4° = **90** people in total.

b) Blue: 25 × 4° = **100°**
White: 152° ÷ 4° = **38 people**
Other: 11 × 4° = **44°**

c)
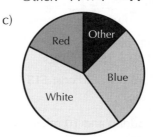

4) Pirates: $\frac{1}{6}$ so 360° ÷ 6 = 60°
Ninjas: 25% = $\frac{1}{4}$ so 360° ÷ 4 = 90°
Zombies: $\frac{12}{36} = \frac{1}{3}$ so 360° ÷ 3 = 120°
Didn't dress up: 360° – 60° – 90° – 120° = 90°

5) a)

b) During week 6, the alpaca's weight
stayed the same, at 40 kg.

c) The lines cross between week 3, and
week 4. So the llama and the alpaca
weighed the same at some point during
the **fourth week**.

6) 20 × 23.4 = **468 seconds**

7) Total weight of men = 6 × 84 = 504 kg
Total weight of women = 5 × 55 = 275 kg
Combined weight = 504 + 275 = 779 kg
So the total weight **is not above** the maximum
weight.

8) Total of all values = 5 × 9 = 45
Missing value = 45 – (8 + 3 + 19 + 13) = **2**

Glossary

area	The area of a shape is the <u>amount of surface</u> it covers.
axis/axes	The <u>horizontal axis</u> (x axis) is the line that goes <u>across</u> a graph or chart from the origin. The <u>vertical axis</u> (y axis) is the line that goes up and/or down from the origin. <u>Axes</u> is the word for more than one axis.
common factor	A factor that is <u>shared</u> by <u>two or more</u> numbers. For example, 4 is a common factor of 8 and 12.
common multiple	Multiples that <u>two or more</u> numbers <u>share</u>. For example, 15 is a common multiple of 3 and 5.
coordinates	They tell you the <u>position</u> of a point on a grid. For example, (3, 4) means 3 units to the right of the origin and 4 units up. The first number is the <u>x-coordinate</u> and the second number is the <u>y-coordinate</u>.
cubic centimetre	A unit for measuring <u>volume</u>, written <u>cm</u>^{3}. A cube with sides 1 cm long.
decimal places	The places in a number to the <u>right</u> of the decimal point (<u>tenths</u>, <u>hundredths</u>, <u>thousandths</u>, etc). The number 4.56 has 2 decimal places.
decimal point	The <u>dot</u> you write between the <u>units</u> and the <u>tenths</u> in a decimal number.
denominator	The <u>bottom</u> number of a fraction.
diagonal	A diagonal line is the line joining <u>two corners</u> that <u>aren't</u> next to each other in a shape. People also say 'a diagonal line' to mean a <u>sloping line</u> (not horizontal or vertical).
diameter	The distance <u>across a circle</u>, passing through the <u>centre</u>.
difference	The difference between two numbers is the <u>bigger number – smaller number</u>.
divisor	The number that <u>divides</u> into another number.
enlargement	An enlargement is where a shape gets <u>bigger</u> using a <u>scale factor</u>.
equation	Something like <u>A + 6 = 7</u> or <u>A + B = 3</u>, with a mathematical statement either side of the equals sign.
equilateral triangle	A triangle with <u>all sides the same length</u> (and all angles 60°).
equivalent	Something that has the <u>same</u> value but looks different. For example, $\frac{1}{2}$ and $\frac{2}{4}$ are <u>equivalent fractions</u>.
estimate	An estimate is a <u>sensible guess</u> at the answer. You can use <u>rounding</u> to help you estimate answers.
exterior angle	An angle between <u>one side</u> of a shape and a <u>line</u> extended from the <u>next side</u>.
face	A <u>side</u> of a solid shape. Faces can be <u>flat</u>, as on cubes. They can also be <u>curved</u>, as on cylinders.

Glossary

factor	A whole number that <u>divides exactly</u> into another whole number. For example, the factors of 6 are 1, 2, 3 and 6.
formula	A formula tells you how to work out <u>one quantity</u> when you know a <u>different quantity</u>. E.g. Volume of cuboid = length × width × height.
horizontal	Going <u>across</u>. This line is horizontal. ⟹ _____ Shelves and table tops are horizontal.
image	A <u>transformed</u> shape.
improper fraction	A fraction with a numerator <u>bigger</u> than its denominator, e.g. $\frac{9}{7}$.
interior angle	An angle <u>inside</u> a shape between two adjacent sides.
irregular polygon	In an irregular polygon, the sides are <u>not</u> all <u>equal lengths</u> and all angles are <u>not</u> the same.
isosceles triangle	A triangle with <u>two</u> equal sides and <u>two</u> equal angles.
line graph	A graph with points that are <u>joined</u> by <u>lines</u>.
line of symmetry	If you <u>fold</u> a shape along a line of symmetry, the two halves <u>fit exactly</u> on top of each other. It's the same thing as a <u>mirror line</u>.
mean	One kind of <u>average</u>. To work out the mean, you add up all the values then divide by the total number of values.
mirror line	The same as a <u>line of symmetry</u>.
mixed number	A number that has a <u>whole-number part</u> and a <u>fraction part</u>, e.g. $3\frac{1}{10}$.
multiple	Multiples are the <u>answers</u> in a times table. E.g. multiples of 6 are 6, 12, 18...
net	A <u>2D shape</u> that will <u>fold up</u> to make a <u>solid</u> shape.
numerator	The <u>top</u> number of a fraction.
origin	Where the two <u>axes</u> of a graph <u>meet</u>. It has the coordinates (0, 0).
parallel	Parallel lines, faces and edges are always the <u>same distance apart</u>. They will <u>never meet</u> or <u>cross</u>.
partition	<u>Split</u> a number up. You can partition numbers in many ways. For example, 173 = 100 + 70 + 3 or 173 = 150 + 20 + 3.
perimeter	The <u>distance</u> around the <u>outside</u> of a shape.
pie chart	A circular chart that shows things as <u>proportions</u>. The angles of the sectors in a pie chart add up to <u>360°</u>.
polygon	A <u>2D</u> (flat) shape with <u>straight sides</u>.

Glossary

prime	A prime number is a number that has exactly two factors: 1 and itself. For example, 2, 3, 5, 7, etc.
proper fraction	A fraction that's less than 1. The numerator is smaller than the denominator — for example, $\frac{2}{5}$ or $\frac{3}{4}$.
proportion	Another word for fraction. For example, 1 in every 4 is the same as $\frac{1}{4}$.
quadrilateral	A flat shape with 4 straight sides.
radius	The distance from the centre of a circle to the edge.
ratio	A ratio is one way of comparing amounts. For example, if there are three apples and two oranges in a bowl, the ratio of apples to oranges is 3 to 2, written 3:2.
reflective symmetry	A shape has reflective symmetry if you can draw a mirror line on it.
regular polygon	In a regular polygon, all the sides are equal lengths and all the angles are the same.
remainder	What's left over when you divide. For example, 7 ÷ 2 = 3 remainder 1. The remainder can be written as a number, a fraction or a decimal.
rounding	Finding a nearby number that's similar, but easier to use in calculations. For example, 278 rounded to the nearest 100 is 300.
scale factor	The number each side of a shape is multiplied by in an enlargement.
sequence	A list of numbers or shapes. There is a rule or pattern that links each number or shape to the one before. For example, 3, 6, 9, 12...
simplifying	Simplifying a fraction means making an equivalent fraction with the smallest numbers possible. For example, $\frac{6}{8}$ simplifies to $\frac{3}{4}$.
square centimetre	A unit for measuring area, written cm². A square with sides 1 cm long.
term	Each number in a number sequence. For example, in the sequence 0, 2, 4, 6, 8, there are 5 terms.
tessellation	When shapes fit together exactly with no gaps or overlaps.
translation	When a shape moves from one place to another without rotating or flipping.
vertex/vertices	A vertex is a corner. Vertices is the word for corners.
vertical	Going straight up and down. Walls and flag poles are vertical.
vertically opposite angles	Pairs of angles made when two lines cross. Vertically opposite angles are equal.
volume	The volume of a shape is the amount of space it takes up.

Index

2D shapes 50, 53
3D shapes 51, 52

A

adding fractions 18
angles 55, 56
area 44-46, 54
axes 57-59

B

BODMAS 11
brackets 11

C

calculation problems 13
checking calculations 10
circles 54
common denominators 18
common factors 12
common multiples 12
conversion factors 42, 43
converting between fractions,
    decimals and percentages
    24, 25
converting units 42, 43
coordinates 57-59
cross multiplying 16
cubes 47, 51, 52
cuboids 47, 52
cylinders 51

D

decimals 22-25
denominators 16-20, 24, 32
diameter 54
dividing 8, 9
    by 10, 100 or 1000 21
    decimals 22
    fractions 20
drawing
    line graphs 64
    nets 51, 52
    pie charts 63
    triangles 50

E

edges (of a shape) 52
enlargements 30
equilateral triangles 53
equivalent fractions 16, 17, 32
estimating 10, 22
exterior angles 55

F

faces (of a shape) 51, 52
factors 12
formulas 39
fractions 16-20, 24, 25, 32

I

improper fractions 18, 20
interior angles 55

L

line graphs 64
long division 8
long multiplication 7

M

maps 29
mean (average) 65
mental maths 9
mirror lines 58
missing number problems 37, 38
mixed numbers 18, 20
multiples 12
multiplying 7, 9
    by 10, 100 or 1000 21
    decimals 22
    fractions 19

N

negative numbers 4, 5
nets 51, 52
number lines 2, 17
number problems 5
numerators 16, 19

O

ordering fractions 17

P

parallelograms 45, 55
pattern sequences 39
partitioning 9
percentages 25, 31, 32
perimeters 46, 54
pie charts 62, 63
place value 2
polygons 53
prime numbers 12
proportions 19, 25, 33, 62, 63
pyramids 51

Q

quadrants 57
quadrilaterals 53, 55

R

radius 54
rectangles 46
recurring decimals 24
reflections 58
remainders 8
rhombuses 55
rounding
    decimals 10, 23
    whole numbers 3, 5, 10

S

scale factors 30
scaling 28-30
sectors 63
sequences 36, 39
simplifying fractions 16
squares 53
subtracting fractions 18

T

tessellations 53
time 43
translations 59
treasure map 29
triangles 44, 50, 53, 55

U

unequal sharing 33
units (measuring) 42, 43

V

volume 47

X

x-axis 58

Y

y-axis 58